WOMEN AND INTERNATIONAL PEACEKEEPING

THE CASS SERIES ON PEACEKEEPING

ISSN 1367-9880

General Editor: Michael Pugh

This series examines all aspects of peacekeeping, from the political, operational and legal dimensions to the developmental and humanitarian issues that must be dealt with by all those involved with peacekeeping in the world today.

1. *Beyond the Emergency: Development within UN Missions*
   edited by Jeremy Ginifer

2. *The UN, Peace and Force*
   edited by Michael Pugh

3. *Mediating in Cyprus: The Cypriot Communities and the United Nations*
   by Oliver P. Richmond

4. *Peacekeeping and the UN Agencies*
   edited by Jim Whitman

5. *Peacekeeping and Public Information: Caught in the Crossfire*
   by Ingrid A. Lehman

6. *US Peacekeeping Policy under Clinton: A Fairweather Friend?*
   by Michael MacKinnon

7. *Peacebuilding and Police Reform*
   edited by Tor Tanke Holm and Espen Barth Eide

8. *Peacekeeping and Conflict Resolution*
   edited by Oliver Ramsbotham and Tom Woodhouse

9. *Managing Armed Conflicts in the 21st Century*
   edited by Adekeye Adebajo and Chandra Lekha Sriram

Women and International Peacekeeping

Editors

LOUISE OLSSON
Uppsala University

TORUNN L. TRYGGESTAD
Norwegian Institute of International Affairs

FRANK CASS
LONDON • PORTLAND, OR

First published in 2001 in Great Britain by
FRANK CASS PUBLISHERS
Crown House, 47 Chase Side, London N14 5BP

and in the United States of America by
FRANK CASS PUBLISHERS
c/o ISBS, 5824 N.E. Hassalo Street
Portland, Oregon 97213-3644

Website http://www.frankcass.com

British Library Cataloguing in Publication Data

Women and international peacekeeping / editors, Louise Olsson, Torunn L. Tryggestad.
p. cm. – (The cass series on peacekeeping, ISSN 1367-9880; [10])
Includes bibliographical references and index.
ISBN 0-7146-5236-9 (hardback) – ISBN 0-7146-8217-9 (pbk.)
1. Women and peace. 2. Peacekeeping forces. I. Olsson, Louise, 1973- .II. Tryggestad, Torunn L., 1968- . III. Series.
JZ5578.W658 2001
355.3′57–dc21 2001003696

Library of Congress Cataloging-in-Publication Data:

Women and international peacekeeping. – (The Cass series on peacekeeping)
1. United Nations – Peacekeeping forces 2. Women and war
3. Women and the military
I. Tryggestad, Torrun L.
327.1′72

ISBN 0714652369

This group of studies first appeared in a special issue of *International Peacekeeping* [ISSN 1353-3312] Vol.8, No.2 (Summer, 2001) published by Frank Cass and Co. Ltd.

Printed in Great Britain by [Anthony Rowe Ltd., Chippenham, Wiltshire]

Contents

Acronyms and Abbreviations

AIDS	Acquired Immune Deficiency Syndrome
ASG	Assistant Secretary-General
BiH	Bosnia and Herzegovina
CEDAW	Convention/Committee on the Elimination of Discrimination Against Women
CIVPOL	United Nations Civilian Police (also UNCIVPOL)
DAW	Department for the Advancement of Women
DOMREP	Mission of the Special Representative of the Secretary-General in the Dominican Republic
DPKO	Department of Peacekeeping Operations (UN)
ECOMOG	ECOWAS Ceasefire Monitoring Group
ECOSOC	Economic and Social Council (UN)
ECOWAS	Economic Community of West African States
Fafo	Fafo Institute for Applied Social Science
FAO	Food and Agriculture Organization
FRAPH	Front for the Advancement of Progress of Haiti
FWCW	Fourth World Conference on Women, Beijing
GA	General Assembly (UN)
GI	Private soldier in the US Army (Government Issue)
HIV	Human Immunodeficiency Virus
ICTR	International Criminal Tribunal for Rwanda
ICTY	International Criminal Tribunal for the Former Yugoslavia
KFOR	Kosovo International Security Force
LLU	Lessons Learned Unit
MICIVIH	International Civilian Mission to Haiti (UNIOAS)
MINUGUA	United Nations Verification Mission in Guatemala
MINURSO	United Nations Mission for the Referendum in Western Sahara
MP	Member of Parliament (UK)
NATO	North Atlantic Treaty Organization
NFLS	Nairobi Forward Looking Strategies
NGO	Non-Governmental Organization
NORBATT	Norwegian Battalion of UNIFIL
NUPI	Norwegian Institute of International Affairs
OAS	Organization of American States
OGA	Office of Gender Affairs (UN)
ONUC	United Nations Operation in the Congo
ONUMOZ	United Nations Operations in Mozambique

ONUSAL	United Nations Observer Mission in El Salvador
OSCE	Organization for Security and Cooperation in Europe
PLO	Palestinian Liberation Organization
PRIO	Peace Research Institute, Oslo
RUF	Revolutionary United Front
SLA	South Lebanese Army
SOFA	Solidarity of Haitian Women (Haitian NGO)
SRSG	Special Representative of the Secretary-General (UN)
SWAPO	South West Africa People's Organization
UNAMSIL	United Nations Mission in Sierra Leone
UNAVEM	United Nations Angola Verification Mission
UNDP	United Nations Development Programme
UNFICYP	United Nations Force in Cyprus
UNHCHR	United Nations High Commissioner for Human Rights
UNHCR	United Nations High Commissioner for Refugees
UNHQ	United Nations Headquarters, New York
UNICEF	United Nations Children's Fund
UNIFEM	United Nations Development Fund for Women
UNIFIL	United Nations Interim Forces in Lebanon
UNMIBH	United Nations Mission in Bosnia and Herzegovina
UNMIK	United Nations Interim Administration Mission in Kosovo
UNOMSA	United Nations Observer Mission in South Africa
UNOSOM	United Nations Operation in Somalia
UNPROFOR	United Nations Protection Force
UNSC	United Nations Security Council
UNSF	United Nations Security Force in West New Guinea (West Irian)
UNTAC	United Nations Transitional Authority in Cambodia
UNTAET	United Nations Transitional Administration in East Timor
UNTAG	United Nations Transitional Assistance Group (Namibia)
UNTSO	United Nations Truce Supervision Organization
USG	Under-Secretary-General (UN)

Foreword

It is one of the most lamentable characteristics of modern conflict that women and girls suffer its impact increasingly and disproportionately. They are seldom either the initiators or the prosecutors of conflicts. And yet they have become specifically targeted, as a way to humiliate the adversary and break the morale and resistance of whole societies. Rape, forced pregnancies, sexual slavery and assault are often used as deliberate instruments of warfare.

Steps have been taken to end the culture of impunity surrounding this lamentable practice. We saw a highly promising example of that in February 2001 in a landmark ruling of the International Criminal Tribunal for the former Yugoslavia, which sentenced men for rape in conflict as a crime against humanity.

But while women often are the first victims of armed conflict, they are now becoming recognized as a key to preventing, managing or resolving it. They can be powerful forces for peace, for the reconciliation of their communities, for bringing war-torn societies back to health.

In March 2000, the United Nations Security Council issued a statement calling for the full participation and involvement of women in all peacekeeping efforts. The following October, the Council held its first open debate on women, peace and security and adopted Resolution 1325, which emphasized the need to increase women's role in peace negotiations and in peacebuilding.

We in the United Nations Secretariat know at first hand the invaluable support women can provide to peace processes in many countries – by forming women's associations, NGOs and church groups to ease tensions; by communicating across political affiliations and ethnicity; and by working to persuade men to accept peace. We must build on these experiences to integrate women more effectively in peace processes worldwide. We must integrate women's efforts in all our peace strategies, and capitalize on the beneficial role women can have in both conflict resolution and peacebuilding. But we will be better at this if we have enough women in key positions. Clearly, the UN must make determined efforts to increase the numbers of women in peacekeeping operations, especially at the senior levels. Following the recommendations of the Brahimi Report, a senior appointments group is being organized, consisting of representatives from key departments and entities whose tasks will include advising the Secretary-General on the selection of women for senior mission posts.

I am heartened, therefore, that this volume is devoted to the subject of women and peacekeeping. It will be valuable in furthering the understanding that women's full participation in managing, preventing and resolving conflicts is essential for the maintenance and promotion of peace and security in the 21st century.

LOUISE FRÉCHETTE
Deputy Secretary-General of the United Nations
with responsibility for spearheading internal reform

Introduction

LOUISE OLSSON and TORUNN L. TRYGGESTAD

On 31 October 2000 the United Nations (UN) Security Council adopted Resolution 1325, which recognized the urgent need to mainstream gender perspectives[1] into peacekeeping operations, the importance of specialized gender training and the need to understand the impact of armed conflict on women and girls. This was the first time in the UN's history that the Security Council formally decided on a gender issue. Moreover, in a statement made on International Women's Day, 8 March 2000, members of the Security Council recognized that peace was inextricably linked with equality between women and men. They then went on to affirm that equal access to and full participation of women in power structures and their full involvement in all efforts for the prevention and resolution of conflicts were essential for the maintenance and promotion of peace and security.[2]

Both the statement and the resolution can be understood as a final reward for the efforts made by determined women who have fought for equality between women and men in UN contexts since the organization's founding in 1945. One of the pioneering women was Eleanor Roosevelt. As one of the state representatives drafting the Charter, she expressed the view that the experiences from World War II underlined the need to include equality between the sexes (as opposed to equality between men only) in the Charter. In an open letter to the Women of the World, presented to the first Assembly of the United Nations on 12 February 1946, she stated: 'This new chance for peace was won through the joint efforts of men and women working for common ideals of human freedom at a time when the need for joint effort brought down barriers of race, creed and sex'.[3]

Eleanor Roosevelt's analysis continues to be valid, particularly with regard to contemporary conflict and post-conflict situations. However, this perspective has not been reflected in how multifunctional peacekeeping operations have been constructed or implemented. The majority of conflict situations in which the UN intervenes today are of such a complex nature that the joint efforts from both men and women are required to handle conflict and to make such operations as effective as possible according to their mandates. In many instances good relations with the civilian population are a prerequisite for effective peacekeeping; good relations with the local population often imply easy access to information at the grass roots level and increased security for both the UN personnel and the local population. In local societies where women and their dependants often constitute the majority of the population, it is an advantage to have a large number of women in various peacekeeping capacities. In such situations experience indicates that it is easier for female peacekeepers to establish a dialogue with local civilians than it is for their male colleagues.

An increased number of female peacekeepers also mitigates such security procedures as body searches of women. This is particularly important with regard to preventing the smuggling of weapons and explosives. A more balanced number of male and female peacekeepers would also tend to reduce the level of sexual harassment and violence against local women – a problem that has been steadily growing throughout the 1990s. It is a general assumption that an increased number of female peacekeepers would benefit all aspects of the operation through the greater variety of experiences these women would add.

The apparent gendered aspects of modern-day peacekeeping, held together with gender-blind missions such as the ones to Mozambique and Cambodia, have gradually placed gender on the agenda of the various departments and units dealing with peace and conflict issues within the UN system. The process has, however, been a slow one, entangled in both institutional inertia and outspoken resistance among member states. Finally, after a long period of planning and discussions, a comprehensive study was initiated. Entitled *Mainstreaming a Gender Perspective in Multi-dimensional Peace Support Operations,* it was launched by Angela King, the UN Special Advisor to the Secretary-General on Gender Issues and the Advancement of Women at a workshop held at the Department of Peace and Conflict Research in Uppsala, Sweden, in June 1999. The Lessons Learned Unit within the UN Department of Peacekeeping Operations (DPKO) took on the main responsibility for the study. Focusing on previous UN peacekeeping missions, such as the missions in Namibia, El Salvador and South Africa, as well as the ongoing mission in Kosovo, the aim was to gain insight with regard to gender. The study resulted in the Windhoek Declaration and the Namibia Plan of Action (see appendices to this collection) as well as a report that was presented to the Beijing +5 General Assembly meeting in New York in June 2000. The study contributed to placing the issue of gender and peacekeeping on the agenda of the Security Council, to which Resolution 1325 bears evidence.

Parallel to this study and its related activities, the Expert Panel on United Nations Peace Operations[4] was also working on what would later be known as the Brahimi Report. The mandate of this expert panel was to present 'a clear set of recommendations on how to do better in future in the whole range of United Nations activities in the area of peace and security'.[5] The report was released in August 2000. However, for the many people committed to gender mainstreaming and who thought that time was ripe for some substantive policy influence, the Brahimi Report was a striking disappointment. The only reference made to gender in the Brahimi Report was found in the concluding chapter on 'Challenges to implementation' and was linked to the conduct of UN personnel in the field. The report advised that 'they must also treat one another with respect and dignity, with particular sensitivity towards gender and cultural differences'. The complete disregard for the apparent gendered aspects of current peacekeeping operations and the women involved (both locals and as peacekeepers) no doubt bordered on the offensive not only for those involved in the study itself, but also for those women who are engaged in peacekeeping operations. In that respect the Brahimi Report proved to be yet another example of how gender issues have been treated throughout the history of the organization: so-called 'women's issues' have historically been marginalized from the mainstream activities of the UN regardless of the obvious gendered implications.

* * *

This brings us to a discussion of the term 'gender' in relation to this collection's focus on women and peacekeeping. Gender is a wide term, originating in the assumption of socially constructed femininities and masculinities. The term is relational in the sense that you cannot define or discuss femininity without also having an idea of masculinity and vice versa. Thus, when discussing gender perspectives the term ideally should include the perspectives of both women and men. It also entails a society's social power relations. Gender perspectives have often been utilized to critique what has been considered a male-dominated research agenda and underline the obvious gaps of knowledge that result when half a population's ideas and roles are disregarded.[6] As there is a wide gap in the knowledge concerning women and peacekeeping – as opposed to men and peacekeeping – this collection is devoted to shedding light on the former. This does not in any way exclude other important aspects of gender and peacekeeping. It simply addresses the need to broaden our views by indicating certain areas where a gender perspective provides additional valuable information to peacekeeping research. The various essays in this collection all display alternative approaches to peacekeeping analysis – hopefully in a manner that will broaden our understanding of the complexity of peacekeeping.

Mary-Jane Fox offers an introduction to the idea of women and peacekeeping and its history. It is commonly held that this idea is new and, consequently, that we cannot expect to see any immediate changes. However, Fox's essay argues that 'the relatively recent concept and practice of peacekeeping have been a predominantly male concern, in the same way as war and military matters in general. Efforts to introduce gender mainstreaming into peacekeeping missions are notable, yet they are long overdue, since they are hardly a new idea.' The essay then makes use of the statement 'even the ancient Greeks', which is often used to support contemporary arguments through historical justification. In this essay, two ancient Greek plays, *Antigone* and *Lysistrata*, challenge both past and contemporary objections to women's involvement in matters of peacekeeping as well as the negative stereotyping of women upon which those objections are based. Still relevant in today's world, *Lysistrata* in many instances is even believed to be an actual historical event, and it is frequently cited. A prominent example of reference to the play was made by Nelson Mandela concerning women's role in the conflict resolution process in Burundi, a successful effort by women. *Antigone* raises, amongst others, the issue of human rights in situations of war. The main character, Antigone, must justify not only why her soldier brother, fighting on the enemy side, has the right to be buried, a right today established in international law, but also the fact that she, as a woman, takes a decision which transgresses into the public sphere. The decision transforms her into a potent actor in the sole domain of men. Moreover, both plays have in common that each of their lead women helps to put a human face to one of the most inhuman of situations: war.

Moving closer to modern-day peacekeeping, Gerard DeGroot's contribution discusses women's roles in the military throughout history and the implications of this for women in peacekeeping operations. The importance of the military in peacekeeping is evident, as these components remain central to UN operations. This is so even if Dag Hammarskjöld's well-known statement that the military is the only body that can do peacekeeping today has to be somewhat amended. DeGroot finds that 'gender stereotypes of peaceful, nurturing women, common to almost all cultures, have traditionally limited the participation of women in the military and in combat. When women have participated in war, by subterfuge or in an emergency, their contribution has subsequently been discounted in order to limit the effect upon gender dynamics.' DeGroot concludes, however, that 'the increased deployment of military units in peacekeeping operations has led to an appreciation of the qualities women supposedly possess – regardless of whether they are genetically or socially determined.' The changing role of the military in multifunctional peacekeeping operations might be one factor which in the future could result in an increased interest in recruiting women precisely because they are women. They are believed to possess important qualities not easily found in men. The work for increased equality in the UN system is another factor that might affect the number of women participating in peace operations. From 1994, the organization began to encourage contributing countries to include more women in their peacekeeping military units.

The inclusion of more women in peacekeeping operations has been a part of the gender mainstreaming agenda during the last few years. This is one of the main topics of Judith Hicks Stiehm's essay. In her capacity as the former consultant to the Lessons Learned Unit's project *Mainstreaming a Gender Perspective in Multidimensional Peace Support Operations*, she provides an overview of the evolution of peacekeeping and the different roles women have served within this particular field of conflict management. She discusses the expansion of peacekeeping into areas of humanitarian relief, refugee return, demining, civilian policing, demobilization, human rights monitoring, elections, and nation building. Stiehm also emphasizes how these new activities directly affect women and women's opportunities for participation in international operations. Further, she emphasizes that women now have an opportunity to direct these new aspects of peacekeeping more in accordance with gender mainstreaming policies. She notes that '[t]o implement and institutionalize these new policies will, however, require commitment, resources, and sound strategies to overcome institutional inertia and, sometimes, resistance'. To overcome the institutional inertia progress with regard to the development of UN documents such as the Windhoek Declaration and the Namibia Plan of Action, as well as Security Council Resolution 1325, are important steps in the right direction.[7]

Henry F. Carey's essay continues the discussion where Stiehm leaves it. His point of departure is international norms and how the new international regime mandating gender mainstreaming responsiveness and women's rights in peace negotiations and complex UN peacekeeping has gradually been consolidated. This regime became legally binding with the Security Council's Resolution 1325 and includes aspects such as the involvement of women's NGOs and individual women in official capacities in peace negotiations and implementation of peacebuilding processes. Carey points out that even though women today constitute the majority of civilian victims and survivors of conflict, decision-making and the implementation of peace agreements still rest with men. In a peacekeeping context this is an interesting observation, especially considering Resolution 1325 and its call for increased numbers of women in peacebuilding. Moreover, Carey's contribution calls attention to the difficulties of implementing norms and makes references to specific failures, such as the impunity for crimes relating to sexualized violence, abandonment by peacekeeping forces, and the isolation of the gender focal point in Sierra Leone. The essay also reviews the record of three peacekeeping missions: Haiti from 1993 to 2000, and the United Nations Development Fund for Women (UNIFEM) projects established as part of the current UN operations in Kosovo and East Timor. To ensure the future success and avoid further failures of UN operations, Carey suggests the 'necessity of NGOs to monitor states and UN bodies involved in peace missions to strengthen the regime's important norms and aspirations'.

The gradual consolidation of norms is also an underlying topic of Inger Skjelbæk's essay. In her survey of the use of sexual violence in times of war, Skjelsbæk claims that even if this particular kind of violence is nothing new to wartime situations *per se*, its extent and strategic importance made it a striking trait of the wars of the 1990s. This was particularly evident in Rwanda and in the Balkans. In these conflicts characterized by ethnic strife, sexualized violence – and particularly rape – became just as important a weapon as machetes and Kalashnikovs. Skjelsbæk argues that 'these acts of violence were part of a new pattern of warfare which the international community did not have an adequate response to'. Acts of sexual violence, which hitherto had been silenced and even defined as 'military necessities', were made objects of immense media coverage in the 1990s. The systematic rape of women horrified world opinion and thrust the issue of sexualized violence onto the international political agenda. Today sexual violence in wartime situations has been recognized as a political criminal act and is mandated to be investigated as such by the International Criminal Tribunals for the former Yugoslavia and Rwanda. According to Skjelsbæk, this recognition is challenging to UN peacekeeping operations: strategies for dealing with wartime sexual violence must be incorporated into policy planning, victims must be assisted in the field, protection from such crimes must be secured and the perpetrators must be condemned and punished.

The importance of integrating gender perspectives into issues pertaining to UN conflict management has been primarily advocated by women. Greater emphasis needs to be placed on the various constructive roles women can play in such instances as peacekeeping operations. This is also debated in the two in-depth case studies in this collection. In the first case study Kari Karamé concentrates on Lebanon and the United Nations Interim Force (UNIFIL). More specifically she reviews the lessons learned from the Norwegian battalion (NORBATT), which served in UNIFIL 1978–98. The Norwegian battalion has been particularly well known for its good relations with the civilian population and its effective peacekeeping. There are of course several reasons for this – and many would argue the presence of female soldiers is one of them. Karamé, therefore, asks the compelling question: 'Do women make a difference?' She looks into the arguments against, as well as the benefits of increasing female participation in peacekeeping. An argument often used to prevent women from participating in peacekeeping operations is the importance of paying respect to local cultures, particularly when deployment takes place in Muslim countries. This was an argument frequently voiced by those opposing female participation in NORBATT. A particularly interesting trait of the local community in the occupied zone in Lebanon was its domination by female-headed households. Further, quite a substantial number of Lebanese women were, in various capacities, actively participating in the war. The Lebanese population was accustomed to women in uniforms, and thus female UN soldiers did not represent an affront to local culture. On the contrary, the female soldiers in NORBATT spent much of their leisure time visiting local women and discussing women's issues. Thereby, Karamé argues, the female staff contributed to a good mission environment as well as an increased access to valuable local information. Moreover, because of the local women's active engagement in the war, it was of great importance to be able to perform body searches of local women at checkpoints. Without the involvement of female UN soldiers this could not have been carried out without disrespect to both the individual woman and the culture as such, and the security of the UN personnel could easily have been jeopardized. Karamé, therefore, argues that women do make a difference.

The question of women making a difference is also an underlying theme in the second case study, which focuses on the United Nations Transitional Assistance Group in Namibia (UNTAG) from April 1989 to March 1990. This was one of the first multidimensional peacekeeping operations with a large civilian UN component. According to Louise Olsson, the UNTAG operation is generally regarded as successful, particularly from a gender perspective. The mission had a fairly gender-balanced staff and was successful in implementing its mandate to the benefit of both women and men. The first building block was thus laid down with regard to developing a gender mainstreaming policy for peacekeeping operations. Olsson argues, however, that the UN lost its momentum. It took another ten years before the UN commissioned a study in which the gendered lessons learned from Namibia were systematically documented. The current process of developing a gender-sensitive UN peacekeeping policy is marked by in-depth discussions about principles and objectives and how these can be operationalized. Olsson points to the fact that many of these objectives were actually put into practice ten years ago in the UNTAG operation without much attention being paid to it. What was particularly interesting about the UNTAG operation was that its much heralded gender policies were not part and parcel of a conscious policy at the leadership level. Rather it was a policy gradually developed and implemented by field staff, predominantly female, who realized that the implementation plan had major flaws with regard to gender-sensitivity. However, the fact that such a substantial number of women were recruited by the leadership to the UNTAG operation seems to have been crucial to its development of gender-sensitive policies and thereby to its success.

The themes of the essays in this volume range from retrospective views on the relationship between women and war in general to analyses of women's participation in contemporary peacekeeping missions. A central topic is how the UN now seems to be developing a policy on gender mainstreaming and how this policy is gradually turning into established international norms. This collection attempts to bring our attention to the many important aspects of women keeping the peace, that is, looking at peacekeeping from a gender perspective.

* * *

The editors of this collection would like to express their appreciation to Michael Pugh, the editor of *International Peacekeeping*, who initiated it, and without whose support the volume would not have become a reality. The contents of the essays are the responsibility of the contributors and we are, of course, much indebted to them for responding positively to our request for essays and for contributing such interesting work. We are particularly grateful to Cynthia Enloe, who agreed to write the concluding remarks. Mary-Jane Fox deserves extra thanks for her support and contribution of ideas and additional editorial advice. The support staff at NUPI, Kirsti Svenning and Eilert Struksnes, also deserve words of thanks for their involvement in the language editing; without them the collection would not have materialized. Finally, we would like to thank Kari Karamé for being a source of great inspiration for those of us who are relative newcomers to the field.

NOTES

1. Gender is a complex concept. During the first decades of the UN, the term 'women' was the main focus of attention rather than 'gender' when issues of equality were discussed. Following a growing understanding of the complex nature of gender relations, and with the introduction of power, the terminology changed. Today the use of 'gender', i.e. the social construction of femininity and masculinity, has in many ways replaced the word 'women' and given the term an inherent meaning of equality. This will be discussed further when introducing the essays.
2. Press Release SC/6816, 8 March 2000.
3. A/PV.29, reprinted in *The United Nations and The Advancement of Women, 1945–1996*, New York: United Nations, 1996, p.104.
4. On 7 March 2000 the UN Secretary-General convened a high-level panel to undertake a thorough review of the United Nations peace and security activities. The panel was mandated to present a clear set of specific, concrete and practical recommendations in their report to the Secretary-General. The panel had ten members with a wide range of experience from peacekeeping, peacebuilding, development and humanitarian assistance. The panel was chaired by Lakhdar Brahimi. The report, known as the Brahimi Report, was presented to the Secretary-General 17 August 2000 (A/55/305-S/2000/809).
5. United Nations Press Release, 23 August 2000.
6. See, for example, Jean Bethke Elshtain, *Women and War*, New York: Basic Books, 1987; Cynthia Enloe, *The Morning After: Sexual Politics at the End of the Cold War,* Berkeley, CA: California Press, 1993; Jill Steans, *Gender and International Relations. An Introduction*, Cambridge: Polity, 1998; and J. Ann Tickner, *Gender in International Relations: Feminist Perspectives on Achieving Global Security*, New York: Columbia University Press, 1992.
7. These documents can be found as appendices to this collection.

The Idea of Women in Peacekeeping: Lysistrata and Antigone

MARY-JANE FOX

The concept and practice of peacekeeping as we know it today is a relatively new phenomenon in human history – no doubt military leaders and warriors from past centuries would be aghast at the idea of a large and well-armed army entering another country *not* with the objective to invade and conquer, but to prevent further bloodshed between two parties. Shocking as that would probably be to our combative forefathers, peacekeeping nevertheless managed to remain exclusively within their domain – that is, the domain of men – and no wonder, since it apparently required military acumen and military might, thus clearly outside the assigned realm for women. In spite of these gender divisions, however, women have of course throughout the centuries made some steps forward, and in this past century, relatively speaking, women can still be seen to have taken some great leaps in matters of peace and war. But in regard to peacekeeping, and from a pan-historical perspective, it has only been mere seconds since the inclusion of women in peacekeeping operations has come into practice, and though the first steps on this road have been predictably rather bumpy, they have also been encouraging.

What is somewhat discouraging, however, is the amount of time it has taken for these first steps and then leaps to come to pass. The idea that peacekeeping and the myriad tasks related to it may well belong within the domain of women as well as men is not an idea from nineteenth or twentieth century feminist thought, Karl Marx, early Enlightenment, or even the extraordinary Renaissance woman, Laura Cereta. Although perhaps the *idea* of women's right to have a say in the life and death matters of war and peace is perhaps as old as *homo sapiens*, the *written* utterances of such matters can be found to have been quite eloquently and indeed cleverly expressed as far back in time as the fourth century BC. The ancient Greeks, with their passion for politics and observing human relations as well as love of the theatre, found the stage to be fertile ground for the exposition of their collective mores and common history. Though there are several plays which, to one degree or another, engage the topics of war and peace, and others which depict the place of women in society, there are few which combine the two, perhaps the best-known examples being Aristophanes' *Lysistrata* and Sophocles' *Antigone*.[1]

For those who are already somewhat familiar with one or both of these plays, they seem to be curious choices; besides the fact that they are both from ancient Greece and both are entitled with the names of their female main character, they appear to have little in common. First of all, *Lysistrata*, to many people, is often viewed as a somewhat bawdy effort, one that appeals to society's lowest common denominator with its at times 'indelicate' language – pedestrian fare, and perhaps not really worth being taken too seriously. It contrasts starkly with *Antigone*, a proper Greek tragedy which in fact is part of an even more tragic trilogy and includes all the inevitable commotion one can bear: leonine courage, high moral standards, unspeakable shame and guilt, regrets and more regrets, self-inflicted wounds and of course, multiple deaths.

But both of these plays speak to us over the centuries because of their universal appeal – they are known and read not only because they survived – for surely not everything which survived has had such appeal – but most importantly, the contents of both plays have provided us with much food for thought, and as such have proven to be richer than what was perhaps their authors' original intentions. However, to that end we will never really know – though many learned people have tried. There is also no limit to the degree to which these and other Greek plays have been painstakingly analysed by Hellenic scholars – from the meaning of various symbols to the dissection and reinterpretation of various words and phrases to the explication of practical historical realities (such as street plans, contemporary laws, and even ancient coinage) – one is hardly at a loss to find literature on the topic.

But what might these plays have to offer the idea of mainstreaming women into peacekeeping operations, or their role in matters of war and peace at all? What might the thrust of these works have to say to the involvement of women in civilian policing, humanitarian law, policy making and negotiating agreements? At first glance, the idea that they offer anything at all on these issues seemed a bit far-fetched, a bit too much of a stretch. But a closer look reveals that while both plays challenge traditional beliefs about women's place in society as well as the public/private dichotomy in which assigned roles are carried out, they also ironically allow us to read firsthand Antiquity's views on female stereotypes – and these stereotypes have survived to the present. It is also interesting that both authors reveal a peculiar prescience on an issue which preoccupies the United Nations today, as well as some intriguing anachronistic perspectives on the paradigmatic nature/nurture, or essentialist/constructivist[2] debate on the essence of gender.

Overview of the Plays

Lysistrata

Aristophones' *Lysistrata* is only one of his 11 comedies that still survive, and is hardly the only play in which he combines the element of politics and war, women taking control, or both, in somewhat absurd circumstances.[3] Its timely first performance in 411BC took place in the context of the closing years of the complex second Peloponnesian War (431–404BC),[4] a 25-year-long intense conflict primarily between Athens and Sparta. More specifically, it appeared on the heels of Athens' bungled attempt in 413 to attack Syracuse – a move that resulted in a most humiliating defeat.

The main character is the Athenian woman Lysistrata, who is weary of her husband being away at war. She convinces other women, including women from other city-states as well as Athens' primary adversary, Sparta, that in order to make them stop fighting, they should refuse their husbands sexually until the men agree to a truce. The women storm the Acropolis and bar themselves inside, thwarting the demands of the local magistrate and his men to abandon their position and their demands. Lysistrata enjoys several central moments in the play where she cleverly explains and defends her position, and she eventually achieves her aim. As the heroine manages this with self-assured remarks and rejoinders backed by a resolve so strong we would no doubt all benefit from its scraps, the reader comes to see her as a naturally skilled negotiator who brings the Athens–Sparta rivalry to its knees.

Antigone

In contrast to *Lysistrata*, Sophocles' *Antigone* was first performed decades earlier, in 442, which was a period of a restive peace between Athens and Sparta, 449–432BC, and between the first and second Peloponnesian Wars. Although border skirmishes and other outbreaks occurred, there was no prolonged war between the two city-states. The first in his series of the saga of Thebes (which subsequently included *Oedipus the King* and *Oedipus at Colonus*), the play became so popular that it has been credited with influencing Sophocles' election to public office. *Antigone,* in fact, won first place in the coveted drama competition held every year at the Festival of Dionysus.[5]

The fated heroine of this tragedy is the strong-willed young woman Antigone, who is one of four offspring of the ill-fated union of Oedipus, her father, and Jocasta, who was her mother *and* grandmother. She and her siblings have been living in the care of her uncle, Creon, who is king of Thebes. Antigone is also engaged to Haemon, Creon's son. She encounters a predicament when she finds that one of her brothers, Polynices, has joined the enemy armies of Argos in attacking Thebes, and has been killed. Although her other brother has also been killed in battle fighting *for* Thebes, Polynices is considered a traitor and according to decree is not permitted or deserving of even a simple burial. Antigone sees the injustice in this and openly states her case; in doing so she stands up to her uncle-king, Creon, as well as the conventions of the day, when Creon makes clear that a woman's opinions in the male business of war was beyond convention, almost forbidden, and certainly not to be tolerated. In maintaining her position, Antigone pays the ultimate price, the same price, in fact, that any combat soldier would do when defending a cause.

Excerpts from Lysistrata

As if it was not bad enough for Aristophanes to be clearly trifling with the sensibilities and conventions of his audience in this play, it is even worse that it is an audience which has changed little in more than two thousand years. He challenges us with the ultimate question about the good of humankind's common polis: *who indeed is best to save the city?*[6] He unapologetically posits woman as humanity's champion, and in no uncertain terms sets about elevating her to a status and capability well beyond ancient Greek (and perhaps even twenty-first century) expectations.[7]

In the opening scenes of the play, the audience finds Lysistrata fretting over the fact that there seems to be a slow response to a meeting of women she has called, a meeting on 'a far from trivial matter' (v.15), wherein 'the salvation of all Greece is actually in the hands of her women' (v.30). Notably, she refers to all Greek women, not just Athenian, and soon enough women from various Greek city-states arrive. Lysistrata proposes to the women that in order to have their husbands at home again – the men are *always* away at war – they need to find a way to make the men stop fighting. The way to do it, she proposes, is for all the women to refuse to have sex with their husbands until they agree to cease fighting. In this, Aristophanes himself seems to be proposing that, in contrast to the hard and fast boundary between private and public, from private considerations the public good can emerge – indeed, even from the private considerations of second-rate citizens, women; the boundary between this division is more fluid than is supposed. Moreover, it is hardly a small contribution the women might be making to the public good, and it might indeed be the ultimate contribution: 'as bringers of salvation and civic order'[8] for all of Greece.

After the women are drawn together, Lysistrata reveals a plan, and it should be little surprise that it involves seizing a public building, and somehow fitting that of all the public buildings there are to choose from, it is the most eminent building in Athens which Aristophanes has arranged for them to occupy: the Acropolis.[9] The women barricade themselves within its gates, and shortly thereafter a confrontation occurs between a chorus of old men, who attempt to smoke the women out of the Acropolis and a chorus of old women have brought water to put out the fire; the old men are doused with the cold water, which seems to have called the attention of the local magistrate, who is accompanied by four policemen. With comments about 'women's licentiousness' (v.388) and 'the sort of unbridled excesses you get from them' (v.398), he unsuccessfully attempts to pry open the gates of the Acropolis and soon encounters Lysistrata face to face. The ensuing argument is memorable: his insults towards the women fly, ranging from 'animals' (v.469) to 'monsters' (v.476) to the suggestion that women have the necessary spirit only for wine-shops (vv.464 and 466) and not to fight for their principles.

When Lysistrata states that the women intend to keep the public's money safe and stop the men from waging war, she is soon asked 'what caused *you* to concern yourselves with war and peace?' (v.503). The magistrate is scolded that besides the squandering of public funds (he is reminded of poor decisions in the past – no doubt a reference to Syracuse), and the unfortunate surplus of unmarried women, there is also the fact that women 'contribute *men*' (v.651) to the city. Ignoring any truth there might be to these arguments, the men decide that this revolt is a conspiracy initiated by their long-time rival, Sparta. Provoked further by an older woman, the men decide to attack, and their leader attempts to rally them by first encouraging them to take off their tunics since 'a man ought to smell like a man right from the start' (v.463). They are further galvanized by the idea that the women need to be seized immediately before they progress any further and excel in the manly art of warfare, where they might 'even build warships, and try as well to attack us with them and ram us … and if they turn to horsemanship, you can forget about our cavalry; there's nothing so equestrian as a woman or so good a mounter, and even at a gallop she won't slip off' (vv.671–9). This appears to be a provocation from Aristophanes that what is military is not necessarily the sole domain of men, and that women would be quite able to perform well in such matters too.

Eventually the men agree to stop fighting, and, interestingly enough, give in for purely *private* reasons (the withholding of sex), their leader commenting, 'Be damned to you! You're such born cajolers, and that old saying is well and rightly said – "neither *with* the deadly pests nor *without* the deadly pests"' (vv.1038–9, italics added). Lysistrata then reminds the gathered Athenian and Spartan men of their common heritage as well as the mutual indebtedness they should feel towards each other. A celebratory banquet is held, and, in keeping with Aristophanes' characterization of men as 'ignoramuses',[10] the audience is privy to a conversation between two Athenian diners, and their thoughts on the social–political advantages of inebriation as well as the deficiencies of male sobriety (vv.1225–36):

> First diner: *I've never seen a party like it. The Spartans really were so charming! And we, in our cups, made very clever partyers indeed.*
>
> Second diner: *Naturally, seeing that when we're sober we go out of our minds. If the Athenians take my advice, in future we'll always go everywhere on embassies drunk. At the moment, when we go to Sparta sober, we at once start looking for ways to muddy the waters. The result is that we don't hear what they say, and suspect them of meaning things which they don't say, and bring home different reports of the same exchanges. But* this *time everything pleased us.*

Moments later, in an exchange between a Spartan and an Athenian, the Spartan offers to dance and sing in honour of the Athenians, and the Athenian replies, 'I do enjoy watching you people dance' (v.1246). Aristophanes' finale speaks worlds, for the final words are from a Spartan, who entreats all present to clap, dance, and sing a song in praise of 'the Lady of the Bronze House', Athena, guardian of the city. But it is not necessarily the goddess Athena he exclusively promotes, since, for a short time, the Acropolis had belonged to Lysistrata as well – a comment indeed on who really is guardian of the polis.

Excerpts from Antigone

Unlike the character Lysistrata, Sophocles has devised for our consideration a woman who takes no public ground, has no allies or bargaining chip, and stands utterly alone in her defiance of the king and his laws. He has fashioned for his audience a rather noble young woman, one whom we can respect and admire, and an admirable contrast to the male characterization of women found in Lysistrata. He has the relative effrontery to posit woman, the inferior household creature of Greek society,[11] as a watchdog for morals and a higher code of ethics, and reminding his audience of all the usual slurs aimed at women, Sophocles boldly makes his character nobler still, as she defends her principles to the death.

The play opens with Antigone informing her sister of their brother Polynices' misfortune in death – that as a form of posthumous punishment, a city proclamation prohibits anyone from burying him, and that his body is deserving only of being left out as 'carrion for the birds and dogs to tear, an obscenity to behold' (vv.229–31). Punishment for such an attempt is public stoning – to death – inside the walls of the city. Antigone plans to bury him nevertheless, citing laws higher than Creon's martial law, 'the laws the gods hold in honour', 'the great, unwritten, unshakeable traditions' (v.504), wherein 'death longs for the same rites for all' (v.584). Antigone is speaking about a right and rite now contained in Article 17 of 1949 Geneva Convention I, which ensures the burial or cremation of all dead, who are in fact to be 'honourably interred'. She plans to at least symbolically bury her brother, despite the reminder from her sister that 'we are women, … not born to contend with men … we're underlings, ruled by much stronger hands, so we must submit to this, and things still worse' (vv.74–7).

Creon is eventually told that Polynices' body has been covered with earth, and launches into a tirade, certain that corrupt people were bribed to perform this forbidden act. Soon Antigone is brought before him as the culprit, and she readily admits her treason while trying to reason with Creon. But Creon realizes that he 'is not the man, not now; she is the man if this victory goes to her and she goes free' (vv.541–2). While arguing with her he proclaims 'while I'm alive, no woman is going to lord it over me' (vv.593–4). When questioned over his decision to put Antigone to death and thus kill his son's bride-to-be, he attests to the reported contemporary value of women by responding, 'Absolutely: there are other fields for him to plow' (vv.641–2) and refers to her as a 'worthless woman' (v.644). He later advises his heartbroken son 'never lose your sense of judgement over a woman … a worthless woman in your house, a misery in your bed … spit her out, like a mortal enemy, let her find a husband among the dead' (vv.723–30). He further underscores his contempt for women by referring to anarchy in the feminine, and rates it as the greatest crime there is. He concludes by stating 'never let some woman triumph over us. Better to fall from power, if fall we must, at the hands of a man – never be rated inferior to a woman, never' (vv.752–61).

As Haemon makes it clear he cannot agree with his father's edict, Creon then turns on his own son, referring to him in such terms as 'degenerate' (v.831), 'soul of corruption, rotten through – woman's accomplice' (v.836), and last but not least, 'woman's slave' (v.848). And Antigone, who is to be sealed up inside a rocky vault, is told by Creon that for her there is 'not a word of hope – your doom is sealed' (v.1026).

He first considers stoning her to death, but it is suggested that the citizens will not support such a public spectacle[12] – not only because her relative guilt or the popularity of his leadership (or both) are in doubt, but also because stoning a woman is, after all, an attack on private life, and stoning such a woman is an attack on the private environment which fostered the very principles on which she resolutely stands. It might also be that Sophocles has something to say about Man's well-established taboo of mixing private and public ... impossible, unthinkable to combine, and perhaps because to do so can be dangerous. Creon decides instead to wall Antigone up in a cave, away from public scrutiny, and as such a more fitting place in which to permanently silence the human creature who is destined by Man to inhabit only the private sphere. What is private should remain so, even in death.

Sophocles seems anxious to show his audience how murky this division really is, how easily one can be mistaken for or disguised as the other. After all, Creon has his pride in mind more than the public good. What's more, Antigone's private death sentence suggests that her private need to bury her brother might not in fact be so very private or so very individual after all, that her private beliefs might in fact be shared by public sentiment, thereby making them a matter of public concern – this blurs the distinction between public and private. In doing so, Sophocles implies to his audience not only that the border between private and public is mutable, but also that the differences between men and women ought not to be so hard and fast either – women too have something to offer the common good, though it may well take the likes of Antigone to prove the point.

What follows is a chain of events and people which truly epitomize the concept of *Greek tragedy*: due to some convincing from the blind prophet Tiresias (whom, the audience soon discovers, is even more 'sighted' than Creon). Then Creon has a change of heart about Antigone's death sentence, but as he is about to release her he discovers that she has already killed herself. Creon's guilt now cannot be assuaged, and as if the death of Antigone was not enough to regret, Creon's broken-hearted son Haemon impales himself on a sword and then his mother, Creon's wife, stabs herself at the altar.

And all this over a young woman who made no great demand: she had not attempted to storm the palace, conquer Thebes, garner an army in her name, or threaten the life of the king; the relatively small demand she had was for her deceased brother, which she understands – and we understand – to be a fair and just universal right. But this relatively small request is nevertheless intolerable and unthinkable – not only because she wants to perform an act which the king does not allow, but particularly because she is a *woman* defying what the king will not allow, because she defies the boundaries between public and private, because she is a threat to the established order. The irony of it all, despite the fact that she is only a character in a play and not a historical personality, is that her death in the tomb makes her come alive to the audience and at the same time become immortal. She survives to the present day because her courage, and, most of all, her message transcends space and time.

Contemporary Thoughts

What do these two works have to say that we can relate to issues in women and peacekeeping today? How do they figure in the integration of women in peacekeeping missions? Perhaps most important is that women in general, regardless of the final outcome of the essentialist/constructivist debate, are powerfully and historically (and pre-historically) bound to those customs, matters, skills, and convictions which have almost invariably been restricted to the private sphere; thus their possible contribution to what is public – in particular matters of war and peace – has been not only overlooked, but as presented in both plays and regarded throughout history, also scorned.

The most shared element between the two plays is that the main characters are posited as the embodiment of what some object to today as the essentialist stereotyping of women. Both Lysistrata and Antigone clearly demonstrate the more positive attributes with which women have been stereotyped: the tendency for discussion, negotiation and compromise; avoidance of more aggressive alternatives; deference to a higher moral authority; and an overriding compassion about the injustices of war.[13] Granted, though Lysistrata's initial interest in ending war has much to do with self-interest, as the play proceeds she is quick to claim other reasons for her actions as well. And although Antigone is not openly against war itself, she clearly is willing to confront the injustice of it put before her. What is also interesting here is that both characters claim their right to having a voice in such matters and neither is afraid to do so. For those who do not support the essentialist argument (which in fact forwards these stereotypes) both Lysistrata and Antigone nevertheless prove to be confoundingly admirable.[14]

The common theme between both plays is that of the hard lines drawn between public and private in ancient Greek society, and the assignment of men and women to them respectively – something which only began to change in the twentieth century. Although both authors dared to present controversy or took risks in having their characters step out of expected social roles and even speak on subjects more or less forbidden to them, it may be more illuminating to say that they did so with zeal and seemed to enjoy it in the process. In stepping out of their assigned 'territory', that is, the private realm, the world of hearth and home, the confinement of domestic life, both Antigone and Lysistrata are not only questioning, but also threatening the political and social order, the accepted status quo. Although Antigone 'merely' stands up to one man, her uncle, King Creon, and Lysistrata and company stand up to the local magistrate and his men, the result is the same: the singular Creon as well as the fighting husbands of ancient Greece are made to look like foolish men indeed, and have much to learn from the likes of women. The playwrights warn men against becoming like the male characters in their plays: Creon, who did not come to his senses until it was too late and lived to regret it all; and the Athenian and Spartan men, who are made to look foolish for bothering with all that unnecessary warfare in the first place.

This also brings us to wonder about the two men behind these plays – just what were they really up to in such a patriarchal society anyway? Almost astoundingly, they offered to their audience women characters who brought a king to his knees or men to the bargaining table. It is impossible to know why they chose a woman to plead the case of a brother's burial, or to do no less than stop an ongoing war. Perhaps they both could well see that women then had 'an unusual kind of authority, a female heroism … that stems from their repeated association with both the day-to-day household economy and with the important civic rituals and cults, upon which the safety of the city ultimately depends'.[15] Perhaps they also were well aware that women are often peacekeepers themselves within the home, and, whether they are so in the home or outside it, they are so on their own and without the benefit of public approval, armies or powerful allies behind them. However, this is only speculation, and it is unlikely we will ever know the rather compelling thoughts and motivations of Sophocles and Aristophanes. But the universal appeal of both their characters is evident as we, the contemporary readers, are drawn into each play and feel as if we have come to know both of them, sympathizing with the defiant Antigone and admiring the tenacity of Lysistrata – we come out the other side wishing we could have met either of the two women, only to remember that they were just characters in a play.

In taking a closer look at *Antigone*, for example, there are several factors in this play which speak to present discussions about women and their role in what is still a man's world, including the world of peacekeeping missions.[16] The first is that both Antigone and the audience are reminded of women's place in society – 'we're underlings, ruled by much stronger hands, so we must submit to this, and things still worse' (vv.74–7). It emphasizes that women are afforded little voice, no power, and few options as to their place in public life, and most particularly so in matters of war and peace – and even concerning something as fundamental as burial of a relative. But this social condition is familiar to women in the present age, too; though we are on the cusp of the twenty-first century, it seems that women's lot in general and their voice in affairs of state have more or less remained unchanged for thousands of years. Indeed there have been some advances in recent decades, but considering how long ago we know such an issue was raised – some 2400 years ago, and in the form of a play, and rather dramatically and successfully – history's progress in this matter has been disproportionately meagre. Perhaps contemporary advances are more fragile than we might assume. In fact, any relative progress made in recent decades might in fact, if care is not taken, only be, in the long run, a moment in time. There is no guarantee that whatever forward movement we can observe this far will continue to move forward – there is good news *and* bad news in regard to gender mainstreaming in peacekeeping – and there are few ramparts to prevent backsliding.

In comparison to *Antigone*, *Lysistrata* provides inspiration against such backsliding, for *Antigone* presents us with a lone woman, victimized by a man, triumphant in death, but dead nevertheless, thereby limiting her victory and her place in what is public. Moreover, it is unclear if Creon had really changed his mind, or if he merely regretted the great suffering he caused. But Lysistrata takes action; she organizes! She brings together different women, convinces them of her plan, seizes control of the Acropolis (unlike Antigone and all Greek women, she *chooses* the place of her confinement to a *public* building!), foils the efforts of the men who try to stop her, and succeeds in actually convincing the men who have been fighting that it is to their own advantage and the advantage of Greece to cease waging war. She is well aware of the repercussions of her plan, and is sure to tell the women and later the magistrate that their mission is no less than to save Greece – and that in fact they will be lauded as Peacemakers of Greece. Hardly a victim, she is a most triumphant woman indeed, for not only has she shown men that women should and must have a say in the affairs of war and peacemaking, but she has also convinced the women – some of whom were reluctant – that they have a right to engage in such matters as well. Lysistrata would have done well at the cusp of the twentieth and twenty-first centuries: with her creative approach to problem-solving, organizational, communication and personnel skills, as well as sense of timing and a good bit of daring and showmanship, she most likely would have organized via the Internet (it would have been the Million Woman March on Washington), taken the US Senate floor (maybe the White House) and been sure to attract lots of media attention.

More than 2000 years ago, however, and even now, two Greek playwrights invite us to consider that women should have a say in matters of war and peace, and that what has been relegated to private is relevant for what has been relegated to public, for private life is indeed upon what public rests and depends. Those very customs, matters, skills and convictions – and the people who harbour them – need to be as much a part of matters of war and peace as guns and ammunition. Lysistrata recognized these shared features among women from all the Greek city-states – would they be that much less shared today? The receptiveness of local women in host countries towards women in the peacekeeping missions would say *no*; and the relative success of the Namibia peacekeeping mission which included a large percentage of women would second this.[17] Women and the traits associated with them can and should contribute to the paths of war and peace, and doing so should allow them to have an influential voice without serving in the traditional male role – as combatants. For whatever reasons, women clearly have their own qualities to offer, and do not need to assume traditional male roles – no matter where *male* role origins lie – in order to contribute to public life. Dag Hammarskjöld's comment 'peacekeeping is too important to be undertaken by soldiers … but soldiers are the only ones who can do it'[18] suggests that the concept and training of a 'soldier' must catch up to contemporary realities, and expand from its narrow 'armed combatant' straitjacket. Peacekeeping as a new phenomenon demands a new type of soldier.

At this point, the idea of what constitutes the public sphere is also expanded from its traditional meaning. In this age of global governance, and advanced communication and technology, what is public no longer needs to be seen as the city-state or even the sovereign state; matters of war and peace concern us all at the global level. Whether they realize it or not, women in UN peacekeeping operations bring with them those aspects of private life which have consequence in their host country and with their mission – they have no choice, for there is no simple and easy shedding of a skin they have worn for centuries. This in turn contributes further towards breaking down the public/private distinction, an unnecessary divide which most likely has prehistoric roots linked with sexual dimorphism and stultifying cycles of lactation and pregnancy. Since the dimorphism is no longer a matter of life and death, and reproduction can now be controlled, perhaps it is high time for our thoughts and actions to evolve accordingly. Waiting an additional 2000 years is not an option.

At first glance, then, there seems to be nothing much new under the sun: considering it is only in the late twentieth century that women began to become institutionalized into matters of peace and war, some of the arguments and slurs we read in *Lysistrata* and *Antigone* have a particularly familiar, contemporary and tiresome ring. But there is still to be found something which is indeed new, and that is not only the fact that the late twentieth century – finally – has provided the field of action and served as the period in which Sophocles' and Aristophanes' messages can be seen to be carried out on an institutionalized scale. What is also new is that this is a task no longer to be undertaken by women (or male playwrights!) alone – from the UN Secretary-General down, the sheer imperative and naked *sense* of women in peacekeeping missions has finally become a very public task, and a task which belongs to us all.

NOTES

1. Aristophanes, *Lysistrata*, Alan H. Sommerstein (ed., transl.), Warminster: Aris & Phillips, 1990; Sophocles, *Antigone*, Robert Fagles (transl.), New York: Penguin Books, 1984. There is also a somewhat different version of *Antigone* by Euripides, though there is no complete and authenticated text extant.
2. In broad terms, essentialism argues that women are inherently, by nature, less aggressive, less violent and more nurturing; constructivists argue that the dichotomous attributes we assign to men versus women are socially constructed gender roles and not biologically determined behaviour.
3. In *Women at Thesmophoria*, also first performed in 411BC, women plot to kill the famed Euripides for his negative treatment of women in his tragedies; the play involves a man disguised as a woman and eventually being detected. More significantly, *Women at the Ecclesia*, written in 392BC, involves women dressing as men and taking over the ecclesia (Athenian democratic assembly) and establishing a more equitable system of rule.
4. The first Peloponnesian War took place from 459–451BC.
5. In fact, 18 of Sophocles' plays were reported to have won first place.
6. Christopher A. Faraone, 'Salvation and Female Heroics in the Parados of Aristophanes' *Lysistrata*', *Journal of Hellenic Studies*, Vol.CXVII, 1997, p.56.
7. Ibid. Faraone notes that Lysistrata singles out 'the men of Athens alone as the weak and helpless individuals in need of personal salvation and the women as the powerful force that will rescue them', p.57.
8. Ibid., p.39.
9. The Acropolis was the most distinguished and certainly the most conspicuous building in ancient Greece, sitting high on a hill overlooking the city, the seat of the cult of the goddess Athena, the female guardian of the city. Aristophanes' selection of the Acropolis was a clever choice to locate the purposes and actions of Lysistrata and the other women, who saw themselves as no less than Greece's 'Dissolvers of Strife' (v.554).
10. Faraone, p.57.
11. The subordinate status of women precluding them from public life in Greek society is well known. See, for example, Susan Moller Okin, *Women in Western Political Thought*, Princeton: Princeton University Press, 1979, where she refers to the Greek traditions towards women as misogyny.
12. R. Seaford, 'The Imprisonment of Women in Greek Tragedy', *Journal of Hellenic Studies*, Vol.CX 1990, pp.76–90 (this note from p.76).
13. For more on this, see DeGroot, this collection.
14. DeGroot points out the irony of the essentialist argument in regard to gender mainstreaming in war versus gender mainstreaming in peacekeeping operations.

15. Faraone, p.39.
16. See Carey, this collection, for a discussion on how gender mainstreaming within the UN has 'not realized its potential'.
17. See Olsson, this collection. For further data on women's participation in peacekeeping missions, also see Stiehm, this collection.
18. DeGroot, this collection.

A Few Good Women: Gender Stereotypes, the Military and Peacekeeping

GERARD J. DeGROOT

In the United States, one of the most outspoken critics of gender integration in the military is Stephanie Gutmann, author of *The Kinder, Gentler Military*.[1] She has managed to tap into a common fear about female soldiers, namely that their presence inevitably means a weakening of a nation's military strength. She claims that the 'feminization' of the American military means that it has become 'so politically correct, so exquisitely sensitive to their troops' feelings, so hostile to their own warrior culture, that they may be unable to defend our interests in future conflicts'.[2] The message is clear: recruit women and lose a future war.

Gutmann proves difficult to ignore because she plays upon widely held gender stereotypes, and because she is a woman. The participation of women in the military and in war has throughout history been limited because of those stereotypes. Women, it is held, do not make good soldiers because they are weak, both physically and emotionally. While the physical barriers to participation have been gradually eroded, due to the advent of highly technological weaponry and the improved fitness of women, the emotional barriers remain strong. It is still widely believed that women are genetically programmed for a caring role and cannot therefore summon the aggressive impulses necessary for effective soldiering.

Supporters of gender integration in the military argue that essentialist theories about peaceful women have no validity. The capacity for violence, they argue, is socially, not genetically, determined. This being the case, it should be possible to train women to become effective soldiers, just as it is possible to train men to do so. These campaigners cite random incidents from the past when women, usually as a result of military emergency, have assumed a combat role and have performed effectively.

While the two sides in the debate battle it out with their incompatible theories and statistics, time itself marches on. There is a distinct possibility that the issues which have provoked such strident debate will be rendered moot by the changing nature of the modern military. While war remains depressingly common, a great number of nations do not anticipate being called upon to fight an aggressive war. In these countries, the role of the military has changed, with peacekeeping and disaster relief becoming the most common reason for deployment.

This new role for the military has thrown the question of gender integration into even greater confusion. Stated simply, the gender stereotypes which previously acted as a barrier to female participation in war might actually enhance the potential for women in the military of today. The attributes commonly associated with women, namely a gentle nature, conciliatory attitude and the ability to control aggression, might make them effective peacekeepers – possibly even more effective than men. This means that those who have consistently argued against female participation in the military are suddenly finding that the logic of their argument in fact points toward greater gender integration. On the other hand, those who have struggled hard to attack the stereotypes which have prevented female participation, suddenly find that those stereotypes point to an important contribution which women can make. It is quite possible that, in future, the military will want more women for the very simple reason that they are women.

Women and the Martial Culture

During the French and Indian Wars (1755–65), Martha May, a camp follower attached to the British Army, wrote to Lieutenant Colonel Henry Bouquet, commander of her husband's unit. May, pleading for leniency after an unknown act of insubordination, wrote: 'I have been a Wife 22 years and have Traveld with my Husband every Place or Country the Company Marcht too and have workt very hard ever since I was in the Army.'[3] What is interesting about the incident are the overt indicators of May's sense of membership. Like any male soldier, she was subject to military discipline, but she also felt that her long record of devoted service to the unit entitled her to lenient treatment. She felt herself 'in the Army'.

The Martha May incident demonstrates that the participation of women in the military and in war is nothing new. While formal auxiliary units composed of women are largely a twentieth-century phenomenon, women have been performing support functions throughout the history of warfare. In early modern Europe, women were considered essential to a unit's effective operation, especially since the functions they performed allowed male soldiers to concentrate upon combat. In 1776, the Berlin Garrison of Frederick the Great consisted of 17,056 men, 5,526 women and 6,622 children.[4] The camp follower, often seen as a parasite on the military body, was in fact an essential link in the logistical chain.

Since these women and children lived in camps or barracks with the soldiers, they were directly subjected to, and a part of, the martial culture.

Granted, the women's duties – such as nursing, cooking, carrying water, removing the wounded – were logical extensions of their domestic chores. But they were no less essential for being traditionally female tasks. Molly Pitcher, the feminist icon who supposedly fired a cannon during the American Revolutionary War, may not have been a real individual but rather a mythical archetype which represents those women who serviced the needs of male soldiers. Her name was perhaps an expression of the function she performed, namely that of water carrier.[5]

The professionalization of the military in the nineteenth and twentieth centuries meant that the support functions women habitually performed were taken over by men. In the process, these functions were given a legitimacy never accorded when women did them. A man who carried ammunition, nursed soldiers, or cooked for an army in the First or Second World War was still considered a soldier, in a way that a woman who once did so never was. What gave the man this soldierly identity was his masculinity. Because he was a man, he had a theoretic eligibility for combat, even though he might never actually fight. Because men could kill, they were soldiers. Because women were not supposed to kill, they could never be soldiers. This distinction has continued to the present day: the man who serves as an entertainment officer for a military unit far from the front has little difficulty demonstrating his right to be called a soldier, whereas the woman who serves as a nurse at a casualty clearing station has continually to suffer doubts about her soldierly identity.

Back when physical strength was a prime determinant of military prowess, the potential to kill seemed a predominantly male characteristic. With the passage of time and the development of increasingly powerful weapons which do not require brute strength to wield, that distinction has become ever more contrived. But it has not lost its power. It has remained an important element in the patriarchal distribution of power. Witness, for instance, the enormous advantage which goes to the candidate in a US presidential election who has served in combat. In Israeli society, despite the fact that female service is well-established, combat veterans are favoured in the contest for coveted civilian appointments. Since men alone serve in combat, women suffer a distinct disadvantage.[6]

Throughout history, women have, occasionally, seized opportunities to fight. Some found themselves thrust into the fray by odd circumstance, while others gained entry by subterfuge, often by disguising themselves as men. But because these exceptions were rare, they could be dismissed as unrepresentative. They did not threaten gender distinctions which stemmed from the combat exclusion. Some of these women were fascinating, others admirable, but all were freaks. Neither Joan of Arc nor the fabled women who dressed as men in order to fight in the American Civil War were considered sufficiently normal to overturn patriarchal precepts. And, the fact that a few women disguised themselves as men in order to fight merely demonstrates how gendered the military was. Participation in combat was closed to women unless they could effectively become men.

Feminist historians have often bought into this arbitrary distinction by paying homage to these anomalies, apparently unaware of the fact that, by doing so, they have merely demonstrated that the exception proves the rule. Because these extraordinary women were freaks, they have not made a convincing case for granting status to the multitude of 'normal' women who show no such inclination to challenge gender boundaries in such spectacular fashion. For instance, Trieu Thi Trinh, a mythical nine foot tall Vietnamese giantess who rode into battle against the Chinese in the third century AD upon a massive elephant with her pendulous breasts slung over her shoulders, is a safe heroic icon precisely because few women share her physiognomy.

In other words, there is great danger in eulogizing mythical women, especially those who became men. The key to attacking the combat-based standard of social capital lies in disputing the system of measurement, not in placing disproportionate emphasis upon the odd exceptions which, by strange circumstance, have managed to satisfy it. It is true that, in the past, few women ever fought. But it is also true that few men did. The proportion of males in any society who actually serve is tiny, as is the proportion of soldiers in any army who actually fight.[7] Yet all male veterans enjoy the status which combat accords.

Napoleon recognized that an army runs on its stomach, that the key to a unit's effectiveness is its logistics system. Throughout history women have played enormously important roles in looking after armies, but have not been recognized for doing so. The problem lies not in the contribution women have made, but in the standard by which it has been measured. The great tragedy of Molly Pitcher is that she has been remembered because she *might* once have fired a cannon, not because she *was* a camp follower who carried much-needed water to thirsty troops. In fact, the latter function was far more important to the survival of her unit than the former.

Breaking the Combat Taboo

In most Western societies, it is widely accepted that those who give birth should not take life. Thus, David Robertson, MP, one of the most outspoken critics of the campaign for women to be included in the British Home Guard during the Second World War, argued that 'a woman's duty is to give life, not to take it'. To train women to kill was 'abhorrent'.[8] The combat taboo, a convenient method of constraining women, has often been seen as a measure of civilization. In a July 1940 memo setting out the reasons why women should not be more fully integrated into the army, the British Adjutant-General warned 'once we take the step of enlisting women for Army Service there will no longer be any bar to the employment of women for definitely combatant duties … Apart from the Russians no civilised power has yet resorted to the practice'.[9] The fact that the Russians had broken the taboo implied that they were either uncivilized, or extremely desperate, or tainted by communist devilry.

When given the opportunity, women have fought effectively. But because women are not supposed to fight, the instances when they have done so have been carefully camouflaged. During the Second World War, female members of British mixed-sex anti-aircraft batteries participated actively in combat, came under fire, and suffered considerably as a result of enemy action. But because this service threatened the combat taboo, a clever distinction was made so that women could remain, at least in theory, non-combatants. They were prevented from loading or firing the weapons (they merely aimed them) in order to maintain the illusion that they were not actually killing. Strange anomalies resulted: if the battery came under fire a man might subsequently be awarded a medal for bravery, but the woman who stood next to him was not eligible. Since she had not been in combat, she could not be brave.[10]

In Russia, the combat taboo proved unaffordable on two occasions during the twentieth century. During the First World War, women were formed into all-female battalions as a last ditch effort to stave off defeat and to buttress the Provisional Government. On 9 July 1917, the First Russian Women's Battalion of Death went into action and acquitted itself well. The battalion impressed senior male commanders and embarrassed German troops who surrendered to them. But, after the war, the incident was quickly forgotten. Amnesia became official Soviet policy.

In the Second World War, the Soviets turned in desperation to women after the Germans invaded in June 1941. Women served in a number of combat capacities in every branch of service, most noticeably as fighter pilots. Despite being deployed in antiquated aeroplanes, they performed with great distinction. The women displayed the requisite ruthlessness and bravery in dogfights and, as with any such unit, suffered terrible casualties. But after the war, the nation seemed determined to forget the experiment. Women combat veterans became an embarrassment. Those who wanted to continue their military careers were prevented from doing so and were encouraged instead to return home and have children. Motherhood was presented as a more important and natural service to the state.

After 1945, issues of necessity continued to determine women's deployment in combat. For instance, Vietnamese women were included in communist armies only as a last resort. Though much propaganda value has been derived from the Israeli policy of gender-integrated national service, in truth

Israeli women are not allowed in combat, though, ironically, they are used to train men to fight. In the 1990s the combat taboo was gradually eroded, with women making some significant progress in Western militaries, especially the United States, Canada and the Scandinavian countries. But though American women are currently trained as fighter pilots, they remain excluded from service in ground combat units. In almost every country, the question of how and where women should be deployed inspires strident debate.

Though combat remains predominantly the preserve of males, the proportion of women in the military has steadily risen. This is in part because, for men, the attractiveness of a military career decreases during periods of economic growth and low unemployment. In practical terms, this means that, as far as the military is concerned, the pool of women's labour is proportionately larger and the quality of the female recruit oftentimes higher than that of the male. Militaries, particularly in the West, have consequently turned increasingly to women in order to maintain necessary levels of strength. One senior officer in the United States Army, addressing right-wing opposition to female military service, argued, 'These people simply don't understand that the United States would not be able to field an effective army if we were unable to enlist women.'[11]

Generally speaking, though the old auxiliary units have disappeared and women have been incorporated into the regular military, the jobs they perform are similar to those of 50 years ago. In Algeria, for instance, women made their greatest contribution to the war of liberation through nursing, providing food and acting as couriers. Women in the Israel Defence Forces perform traditional clerical and personnel tasks, and, more worryingly, the pretty ones provide status trophies for male senior officers.[12]

The veterans of Soviet aviation reveal how deeply embedded gender stereotypes are. Despite having themselves demonstrated that women could be effective fighters, an astonishing number of them felt that war was simply not the business of women. They believed that women, as the givers of life, should not kill. 'War is not for women; women shouldn't participate … it's against their nature, because women's first purpose is to preserve peace,' one woman argued. Another female veteran felt that 'the very nature of a woman rejects the idea of fighting. A woman is born to give birth to children, to nurture. Flying combat missions is against our nature.'[13] Thus, they signalled an agreement with the still widely held opinion that their service was an aberration – an unavoidable necessity of no relevance to the structure of normal life.

Motivation, Patriotism and Citizenship

Since the early 1970s, military service, and particularly combat, has been seen by some feminists as an important bastion of patriarchy. To knock it down, it seems, would leave the entire edifice of male domination fatally weakened. These 'right to fight' feminists have challenged governments and the military establishment to allow women into areas of combat from which they have heretofore been excluded. But for most feminists the issue is symbolic; few actually want to drive a tank. Thus, the real battles have been fought by proxies; women who want to serve because they love their country or because they are attracted to the thrill of landing a fighter on an aircraft carrier in choppy seas. In fact, women who want to fight very seldom express their demands in feminist terms or seek overtly to advance the cause of women. This is partly because the naturally conservative military is not a very comfortable home for a woman keen to rebel against social convention. The woman who aspires to an active military career often wants only to change a few of the rules regarding where and in what capacity she herself might serve. She otherwise supports the military's role as a guardian of tradition. She wants to fight because she is proud of and seeks to preserve the society in which she lives.

Because women have not traditionally been given an opportunity – through political or military service – to demonstrate their patriotism or devotion to a cause, they have not been seen as real patriots. The testimony of women who served in the auxiliary forces in Britain during the Second World War reveals a deep sense of pride at being given the opportunity to bear the burdens of citizenship.[14] Through service, a sense of belonging emerged. In this sense women who have served in the military have mirrored the motivations of men who eagerly join up in times of war. War provides a unique opportunity for the active demonstration of one's love of country.

Women who aspired to join the British Home Guard argued that their membership was perfectly compatible with 'women's traditional role as guardian of the home'.[15] This was a powerful argument, as it played upon a culturally acceptable form of female violence common to many societies. For instance, in Vietnamese society, an ancient proverb holds that 'When pirates come into the house, even women must take up arms'.[16] At various times, in order to secure the services of women, Vietnamese nationalists defined the home in broad terms as the nation. While the idea that women should defend their homes was acceptable to many, the thought that they might fight abroad in aggressive wars remains deeply abhorrent to most people. After June 1944, the British government debated whether females attached to anti-aircraft units should be sent to Normandy with the allied invasion force. Critics objected that this deployment would transform the women from defenders to invaders. 'Any woman will defend her home', the Labour MP Mrs A. Hardie argued, 'but it is very different when you send her away to other countries. … It is a nice new world that some … picture for the rising generation of women, who now not only have to produce innumerable children but fight wars as well.'[17]

Because participation in war is accorded great prestige within society, women's participation has been either inhibited by arbitrary means or discounted when it plainly occurs. Thus, women have not derived the personal and political benefits from war service that a man would ordinarily expect. This is most evident in conventional wars, where tradition-bound militaries act as a brake upon social change. It would seem that, in consequence, the best hope for female empowerment might lie in unconventional wars or insurgent units where the apparatus for women's exclusion is not well established and the pragmatism borne of desperation might offer them greater opportunity to defy the combat taboo. It is certainly true that women in the French Resistance (1940–45) and in Mao's Long March (1934–36) were more likely to enter the forbidden zone of combat than were, say, their counterparts in the regular French or Chinese armies. But even in these insurgent forces, women in combat were exceptional. Male soldiers (and quite a few women) still felt a profound sense of unease about the idea that women might kill. Those women who did fight did not enjoy the status which went to male combatants. This is in part because insurgency operations often value women as women. In other words, womanly stereotypes are used to mask a sinister intent, a subterfuge which allows women to make a valuable, often deadly, contribution. Thus, the apparently pure-as-snow virgin tapes ammunition to the inside of her thighs and walks innocently past a guard, or the 'harlot' lures an enemy soldier with promises of carnal delights, then slits his throat. Both tasks require great bravery, but both merely confirm that the 'soldier' is in fact a woman, since neither could be performed by a man. The female contribution does not inspire a reconsideration of the patriarchal social order because it neither threatens masculine stereotypes nor contradicts feminine ones.

Women who have trespassed into the military domain have often been redefined and placed in an uncomfortable limbo where they have lost the most admired aspects of femininity but are denied the status accorded male heroes. Those interested in preserving the status quo (not all of them men) were careful to reassert feminine standards in a profound, overt way in order to curb any consequent improvement of women's status. For instance, Soviet women pilots were often 'packaged' in ways which stressed their femininity. Thus they were shown in suggestive, vampish poses outside their aeroplanes, or, alternatively, were photographed knitting between flying sorties – a symbolic reassertion of motherhood, their natural domain. During the last year of the Second World War, auxiliaries in Britain were given time off for Mothercraft lessons, in order to prepare them for and remind them of their natural peacetime role. This practice brings to mind the Amazons of Greek mythology who, according to Ilse Kirk, were transformed into proper women through marriage. In becoming wives and mothers, they were disarmed and made normal.[18]

Thus, it should not be assumed that combat experience automatically grants status and equality to the combatant, regardless of gender. Although Muslim women have served on the battlefield in Iran, Iraq, Syria, Indonesia and Nigeria, their field service has not resulted in their necessarily being granted the same political and economic rights as their male counterparts. In China, no one could rise to the highest level of party leadership who had not served in the Red Army as a field commander or political commissar. In consequence, no women came close to being part of the centre of power. In Israel, again lacking field service, no woman regularly participates in the meetings of the General Staff. Although there were some Vietnamese women in leadership positions, there was fundamental resistance to women in decision-making roles, exemplified by the belief that 'women cannot lead but must be led'.[19]

Clearly, female service has not inspired a redefinition of the qualities of women as a whole or of the masculine nature of war. Women are changed by their military service, but their service has yet to change the military significantly. All this demonstrates that the ability to kill is a very odd distinction by which status in society has been determined: women do not earn coveted status when they demonstrate that they can kill, while men do not have to kill in order to earn that status.

Gender Roles and the Modern Military

Female military service has often been seen as a logical extension of traditional gender roles. Thus, Frederick Treves, surgeon to Queen Victoria, who favoured the employment of women in the Boer War, argued that 'the perfect nurse … is versed in the elaborate ritual of her art, she has tact and sound judgement, she can give strength to the weak … and she is possessed of those exquisite, intangible, most human sympathies which, in the fullest degree, belong alone to her sex'.[20] Those pressing for women's involvement in war argued that these uniquely female talents had application in a theatre of war. Mabel Stobart, who formed the Women's National Service League in Britain after the declaration of war in 1914, did so with the goal of 'forming Women's Units to do women's work of relieving the suffering of sick and wounded'.[21]

The qualities Stobart had in mind had wide application. British women who volunteered as nurses during the South African War were needed because the male nurses had so obviously proved incompetent. Likewise, after the February 1917 revolution in Russia, and the formation of wholly Polish military units attached to the Russian army, women's groups such as the Polish Women's Circle and the Society of Friends of the Polish Soldier were immediately set up to feed and shelter Polish troops because, it was felt, only women could do the job properly. Women were needed on the Long March because they were especially well-suited to the liaison tasks essential to that campaign – specifically, the need to obtain the cooperation of the population in areas through which the force travelled. Because women seemed less threatening than men, they found it easier to obtain the trust of the locals.

Thus, even those who bitterly oppose the idea of women in combat often feel that women have a valuable role to play in the military. Their participation seems logical because there are tasks which women seem to do better than men. For men to dress wounds and peel potatoes seems an unnatural waste of male talent. The most convincing argument in favour of female service has been that it frees men for duties nearer the line, including combat. 'We are here to relieve men for more important jobs',[22] one British woman proudly announced during the Second World War. There are a number of important ramifications of deployment along strict gender lines. First, it institutionalizes the roles of men as warriors and women as carers and thus reinforces the status assigned to those roles. Second, the fact that women release men for combat can cause antagonism between the sexes. An auxiliary has often been seen as a woman who sends a man to his grave.

Since the 1970s, attempts at gender integration in the military have been motivated largely by a spirit of egalitarianism. Proponents have had to negotiate two obstacles: the first being the widespread belief that women should not fight, and the second being doubts about whether women can fight. Though the combat taboo remains strong, the main obstacle to integration today is the belief that women, as the weaker sex, cannot possibly make effective combat soldiers. It is frequently argued that an army, which has the purpose of protecting the nation, is the wrong place to implement an esoteric principle of egalitarianism. This argument has been rebutted in two ways. First, it has been argued that biological arguments concerning the weaker sex are ill-founded, and are merely arbitrary gender norms in disguise. Proponents have, for instance, pointed out that the average woman today is four inches taller and considerably stronger than the average male soldier who fought in the First World War, yet no one ever questioned the latter's qualifications for combat. The second line of argument holds that war itself has become more technologically oriented and therefore less reliant on brute strength. 'We're no longer the charge-the-beach, stogie in the mouth, cussing, hard-drinking, women-chasing, World War II guy', argues Senior Master Sergeant Paula Byrnes of the US Army. 'The more technologically advanced we get, the less overtly brutal we need to be.'[23] Recent experience in Bosnia and Somalia would, however, undermine the logic of this assertion.

It is easy to discount the progress that has been made. The military is an institution designed to uphold tradition. Essentially conservative, it is resistant to change. But it has also always played a significant part in instigating or contributing to social change, for example, in educating the population, or highlighting such issues as the poor diet of many potential recruits. It is well to remember that the racial integration of the military in the United States occurred at a faster pace than in the rest of American society. In most countries soldiers consider themselves the servants of the state and do as the state directs. Military institutions can therefore have a significant impact on gender relations if legislation is used to spearhead change.

Recently, militaries in Western countries have been rocked by a series of sexual scandals. Critics of gender integration argue that these scandals are proof that women do not belong in the military. On the other side of the divide, those in favour of gender integration have used these scandals as proof that the military is a misogynist institution resistant to change. But easy judgements are dangerous. One of the reasons that these scandals have received so much publicity is that the female victims are much more assertive in seeking legal retribution than would have been the case 30 years ago. Furthermore, the determination of the US military to punish offenders does suggest a recognition of its dependence upon women.

The presence of women in a male-dominated environment means that gender relations within the military have attracted both academic and media attention. Incidents of harassment automatically take on a gendered dimension. In 1990 a female first-year student, Gwen Dreyer, was chained to a urinal at the Naval Academy. The suggestive combination of a young woman, bondage, and a scatological, 'masculine' object helped stoke media furore. But the incident is open to contradictory interpretations. Did it represent gendered victimization, provoked in part by the increasing integration of women into the US military? Or did it in fact represent the acceptance of women, through their inclusion in traditional hazing rituals? There is no simple answer to this question, but it points to one of the central issues inherent in women's inclusion in the military: their mere presence creates ambiguity, an ambiguity with which individuals, institutions, states and nations have to engage.[24]

The Future: A New Role for Female Soldiers?

Dag Hammarskjöld, the Nobel Peace Prize winner and second Secretary-General of the United Nations, once said that 'peacekeeping is too important to be undertaken by soldiers'. But, he added, 'soldiers are the only ones who can do it'.[25] Because peacekeeping can be violent, combat training is essential. But the peacekeeper must also be conciliatory and patient. Few conventionally trained male military personnel combine the qualities of soldier and social worker essential to the job. As a result, United Nations operations have been marred by aggressive behaviour that exacerbates tensions.

The contradictions between peacekeeping and conventional soldiering are profound. In most militaries, training accentuates stereotypical male characteristics. The recruit is encouraged to develop strength and aggression, while ridding himself of stereotypical female attributes like sensitivity and compassion. The well-trained soldier is hungry for battle because it is in battle that he asserts his dominance. Yet the peacekeeper is supposed to keep aggression in check and to pursue the path of conciliation. In peacekeeping, violence signifies failure.

Central to this issue is whether men are inherently more violent than women. Circumstantial evidence suggests that they are. The vast majority of violent crimes are committed by men. Bar-room brawls and soccer riots seldom include women. In the past, military training has attempted to develop and channel this male capacity for violence. But controlling it has proved enormously difficult. Soldiers win wars, but they also occasionally commit atrocities when aggression rages out of control, as the behaviour of the Canadian airborne regiment in Somalia demonstrates. The frustration of the soldier unable to use violence eventually boiled over, and the UN peacekeepers engaged in systematic torture of the local population.[26]

The problem of uncontrolled violence also affects conventional military operations. In Vietnam, for instance, nearly 10,000 American soldiers died as a result of accidents or what is called 'friendly fire'. In many cases these fatalities occurred when violence raged out of control or the impulse toward bravery turned into sheer stupidity. Yet most militaries have decided that it is best to encourage blind aggression and bravery rather than run the risk of a soldier who second-guesses himself. The atrocities, it seems, are an acceptable cost of an effective fighting machine.

The Russian experience demonstrates that women can be trained to be aggressive. But the operative word is 'trained'. Women, it seems, are not usually inclined toward violence. When they are violent, they tend to use their violence in a purposeful fashion, for instance to protect themselves or their children. Their aggression seldom rages out of control. Whether this behaviour is the result of social conditioning or biological determinism remains a matter for intense dispute. Whatever the explanation, this pragmatic, highly controlled violence exhibited by women has applications in the modern military context. If women can be trained to exercise aggression, they can presumably also be trained to control their aggression – perhaps more effectively than men.

In other words, the gender-based argument relating to the role of women in the military might have been rendered moot by the circumstances of peacekeeping operations. Proponents of sexual integration in the military have long argued that women are essentially the same as men and can therefore perform adequately in a combat situation. The peacekeeping issue turns this argument on its head. Women, it seems, might be valuable to peacekeeping operations because they are different.

In a crisis, men and women, for whatever reason, seem to act differently. Men sometimes jeopardize operations because they act like stereotypical men. If women tend to act more peacefully and are prone to seek conciliation, then they might be of value to the peacekeeping situation. Essential to this issue is the question of perception. In other words, the way peacekeepers behave is important, but so too is the way the local population expects them to behave. Thus, the presence of a man in a tense situation can be provocative, even if that man has no intention to provoke. On the other hand, the woman tends to calm stressful situations because she is expected to be peaceful. Various studies have, for instance, shown that men react differently to confrontations with male and female police officers. The female officer tends to calm an aggressive male, while the male officer challenges him. The situation often escalates into a contest of male dominance.[27]

Male violence might not be instinctive. Instead of men being controlled by the testosterone coursing through their veins, perhaps they are more accurately the slaves of cultural conditioning. If military training can teach women to be aggressive, it might also be able to teach men to be more peaceful and controlled. The problem with male peacekeepers on UN operations is that they often lack the training for the function they are called upon to perform. In other words, disasters are understandable if the UN persists in throwing combat soldiers into unfamiliar peacekeeping situations. To date, the Scandinavian countries are among the few nations in which soldiers are given intensive training in peace support. Canada has also made great strides in this direction – a somewhat ironic fact given that some of the worst atrocities on UN operations were committed by Canadian personnel.

The problem is not just one of training but also recruitment. Often young men join the military because they are attracted to the prospect of combat. For these men, being assigned to a peacekeeping operation where they are not expected to fight is an insult to their manhood. In those countries where participation in peacekeeping operations is voluntary (in particular for officers), it is sometimes difficult to get men to volunteer. This is somewhat strange since, in Western countries, peacekeeping operations are currently a great deal more likely to occur than conventional military operations. Clearly what is needed is a redefinition of the purpose of the military. Such a redefinition seems to be occurring, if British Army recruitment ads are an accurate indication. Designed by Saatchi and Saatchi, these ads have specifically focused upon non-traditional deployments of the military and have given special attention to the role of women.

But the UN's dilemma goes beyond the problem of appropriate training or recruitment. Male soldiers are also prone to sexual violence against civilians. No army is immune to this problem, as Canadian experience in Bosnia and Somalia has shown. Rape is a weapon of war. Some 20,000 women were raped in Nanking in 1937, 110,000 in Berlin in 1945, and perhaps as many as 50,000 in Bosnia in the mid-1990s. Rape allows the soldier to deface the culture of his opponent by, in effect, colonizing the bodies of its female citizens. Rape by soldiers remains high even in times of peace. Thus, within the American military community in Japan, its incidence is three times higher than in a similarly sized group at home.[28]

This sort of behaviour has marred UN peacekeeping operations, as the experience from Somalia demonstrates. Equally worrying is the rise of prostitution and sexually transmitted diseases when UN peacekeepers are present. During the Cambodia operation, the number of prostitutes in Phnom Penh increased from 6,000 to 20,000 while the UN was present, and one participant country found that 25 per cent of its soldiers were HIV positive on their return home.[29]

The UN has, until recently, been a male-dominated organization, rather like the military. As late as 1994 women occupied only 13 per cent of decision-making positions within the UN Secretariat. In the Department of Peacekeeping Operations they constituted just four per cent. It is no wonder, then, that at the point where the functions of the UN and of the military intersect, namely on the ground in the world's crisis spots, women have largely been absent. Between 1989 and 1993, just 1.7 per cent of military peacekeepers deployed by the UN were female.[30]

Yet in almost any conflict 80 per cent of the refugees are women and children. In addition to the problems of rape and prostitution mentioned above, the preponderance of males causes practical difficulties. In many cultures, women are virtually prohibited by social convention from talking directly to male strangers. Yet communication is essential to effective peacekeeping. In Somalia, for example, male soldiers had to frisk local women for weapons. While these searches were necessary, they violated social conventions about men touching women. Nor did it help that they were carried out, according to one official report, in a 'rough, intrusive and humiliating manner'.[31]

In Somalia, a marked difference in behaviour was apparent between combat and support units of the US Army. According to a 1995 article in *Armed Forces and Society*, support groups exhibited a strong inclination to understand the problems facing the host society, while combat groups quickly developed a hostile attitude, particularly when the political situation deteriorated. A desire to apply force, even for mild offences, and to assert dominance was evident. It is perhaps no surprise that the combat groups contained no women.[32]

The support groups were still predominantly male. This raises an interesting point, namely that female participation does not have to be large to have a positive effect. In other words, male soldiers are less inclined to assert their dominance if female soldiers are present. Women seem to calm stressful situations. In addition, a 1995 study for the UN Division for the Advancement of Women (DAW) found that the incidence of rape and prostitution falls significantly with just a token female presence. Stated simply, men behave better when in the presence of women from their own culture.

The most notable UN successes of late – in Guatemala and South Africa, for instance – had a greater-than-normal female presence. In both operations, the proportion of females was just under 50 per cent. In the notorious Cambodian operation, on the other hand, no women were present. There is no evidence that women make better peacekeepers, but a great deal of evidence to suggest that the presence of women improves an operation's chances of success. A better gender balance means that the operation more closely resembles civilian society. Its members are therefore more likely to observe social conventions that define civilized behaviour.

There are, of course, problems with deploying a more gender-balanced force. As one official recently admitted, 'though the UN should be pushing for more women, we're begging, borrowing and stealing to get any troops at all'.[33] There are only a few states able to provide appropriately trained women, among them Canada, the US and the Nordic countries. The UN cannot, however, afford to have its operations dominated by Western militaries. But even in Canada, where the percentage of women in the forces is around 12 per cent, their level of participation in peacekeeping units has consistently been lower than that figure because combat units (in which gender integration is least profound) are usually sent.

A British Army recruitment advertisement shows a woman cowering in the corner of a bombed building. As the film runs, a caption reads: 'She's just been raped by soldiers. The same soldiers murdered her husband. The last thing she wants to see is another soldier. Unless that soldier is a woman'. The advertisement plays upon gender stereotypes that have many feminists tearing their hair. Indeed, the recent integration of women into combat units in many Western militaries has been based on the assumption that stereotypes have no validity, that women can be turned into ruthless killers. But peacekeeping is a practical problem in which gender theory has little place. If women are, for whatever reason, calmer and more conciliatory than men, then they have an important role to play. The UN, in other words, might want its female warriors to remain womanly.

NOTES

1. Stephanie Gutmann, *The Kinder, Gentler Military: Can America's Gender-Neutral Fighting Force Still Win Wars?*, New York: Scribner, 2000.
2. Scribner press release accompanying pre-publication copy of *The Kinder, Gentler Military.*
3. Scott Hendrix, 'In the Army: Women, Camp Followers, and Gender Roles in the British Army in the French and Indian Wars, 1755–65', in Gerard DeGroot and Corinna Peniston-Bird, *A Soldier and a Woman*, London: Pearson Education, 2000, pp.38–9.

4. Christopher Duffy, *The Army of Frederick the Great*, Chicago, IL: Emperor's Press, 1976, p.60.
5. See Linda Grant DePauw, *Battle Cries and Lullabies: Women in War from Prehistory to the Present*, Norman, OK: University of Oklahoma Press, 1998, pp.126–31, for a discussion of the myth of Molly Pitcher.
6. See Dafna Izraeli, 'Gendering Military Service in the Israel Defence Forces', in *A Soldier and a Woman* (n.3 above), pp.270–72.
7. In recent times, the proportion of combat soldiers in an army at war can be as low as ten per cent, as was the case with the American force during the Vietnam War.
8. Penny Summerfield, 'She Wants a Gun Not a Dishcloth! Gender, Service and Citizenship in Britain in the Second World War', in *A Soldier and a Woman* (n.3 above), p.128.
9. Dorothy Sheridan, 'ATS Women 1939–45: Challenge and Containment in Women's Lives in the Military during the Second World War', unpublished M.Litt. dissertation, University of Sussex, 1988, pp.16–17.
10. See Gerard DeGroot, 'Whose Finger on the Trigger? Mixed Anti-Aircraft Batteries and the Female Combat Taboo', *War in History*, Vol.4, No.4, 1997, p.437.
11. Conversation with the author, 31 March 2000. The officer chose to remain anonymous.
12. Izraeli (n.6 above), pp.269–70.
13. See Reina Pennington, '"Do Not Speak of the Services You Rendered": Women Veterans of Aviation in the Soviet Union', in *A Soldier and a Woman* (n.3 above), p.164.
14. See DeGroot, '"I Love the Smell of Cordite in Your Hair": Gender Dynamics in Mixed Anti-Aircraft Batteries During the Second World War', *History*, 1997, pp.77–8.
15. Summerfield (n.8 above), p.124.
16. Gerard DeGroot, *A Noble Cause? America and the Vietnam War*, London: Pearson Education, 2000, p.116.
17. *Hansard*, 24 January 1945.
18. Ilse Kirk, 'Images of Amazons: Marriage and Matriarchy', in Sharon MacDonald (ed.), *Images of Women in Peace and War*, London: Macmillan, 1987, p.31.
19. Karen Turner, 'Soldiers and Symbols: North Vietnamese Women and the American War', in *A Soldier and a Woman*, p.199.
20. Christopher Schmitz, 'We Too Were Soldiers: The Experiences of British Nurses in the Anglo-Boer', in *A Soldier and a Woman*, pp.60–61.
21. Yvonne M. Klein (ed.), *Beyond the Home Front*, London: Macmillan, 1997, p.20.
22. Frederick Pile, *Ack-Ack*, London: Harrap, 1949, p.193.
23. Mark Thompson and Leonard Wood, 'Boot camp goes soft', *Time*, 4 August 1997, http://www.pathfinder.com/@@@QoQodgc...om/970804/nation.bot_camp_goes.htm.
24. My thanks to Corinna Peniston-Bird for this observation.
25. Captain Ingrid Gjerde, presentation to UN conference on mainstreaming gender in peacekeeping operations, Uppsala, 2 June 1999.
26. Howard Schneider, 'Panel Blames Brass for Misdeeds in Somalia', *Washington Post*, 3 July 1997, p.A22.
27. Judith Hicks Stiehm, 'Peacekeeping and Peace Research: Men's and Women's Work', *Women and Politics*, Vol.18, No.1, 1997, p.42.
28. Bruce Shapiro, 'Rape's defenders', *The Nation*, 7 July 1996, http://www.thenation.com/issue/960701/0701shap.htm.
29. Bridget Byrnes *et al.*, 'Gender, Conflict and Development: Volume II: Case Studies: Cambodia, Rwanda, Kosovo, Algeria, Somalia, Guatemala and Eritrea', *BRIDGE report*, No.35, Ministry of Foreign Affairs, Netherlands, 1996.
30. Anita Helland *et al.*, *Women in Armed Conflicts: A Study for the Norwegian Ministry of Foreign Affairs*, Oslo: Norwegian Institute of International Affairs, 1999, pp.78–9.
31. Louise Olsson, 'Gendering UN Peacekeeping, Mainstreaming a Gender Perspective in Multidimentional Peacekeeping Operations', *Report*, No.53, Department of Peace and Conflict Research, Uppsala University, 1999, pp.31–2.
32. Laura L. Miller and Charles Moskos, 'Humanitarians or Warriors? Race, Gender and Combat Status in Operation Restore Hope', *Armed Forces and Society*, Vol.21, No.4, 1995, pp.625–31.
33. Gayle Kirshenbaum, 'In UN Peacekeeping, Women Are an Untapped Resource', *Ms*, Jan./Feb. 1997, p.21.

Women, Peacekeeping and Peacemaking: Gender Balance and Mainstreaming

JUDITH HICKS STIEHM

Looking Back

Prior to 1989 there were 15 peacekeeping missions, one-third of which involved Israel and its neighbours. The United Nations Force in Cyprus (UNFICYP) is representative of the early missions. It did bring fighting between Greece and Turkey to an end, but it did not achieve peace. Even today the island remains divided and the mission (which began in 1964) continues. Annual expenses are around US$50,000,000 and more than 150 peacekeepers have lost their lives there. While peacekeeping did stop most killing and neither side in the conflict 'lost', no incentive to agree to a genuine peace – one that would no longer require the presence of third party peacekeepers – seems to exist.[1]

Three early missions should be noted as foreshadowing recent missions. One was the United Nations Security Force in West Guinea (West Irian) (UNSF) which involved the monitoring of elections. In that case authority over West New Guinea was transferred from the Netherlands to the UN, and from the UN to Indonesia in 1962–63.[2] Two other early missions were involved in civil warfare. One was a 1965–66 mission to the Dominican Republic, the Mission of the Special Representative of the Secretary-General in the Dominican Republic (DOMREP). More important was the large, long lasting (1960–64), multidimensional United Nations Mission to the Congo (ONUC), which cost the lives of thousands of Congolese and more than 200 peacekeepers. It also claimed the lives of Congo Prime Minister Patrice Lamumba and UN Secretary-General Dag Hammarskjöld. Ultimately stability was achieved, although the new government was not widely acclaimed.

Many issues raised by the Congo experience were not really examined until the UN became involved in other civil wars and in other multidimensional missions beginning in 1989. One issue involves how the success or failure of a mission should be determined. Was the United Nations Transitional Authority in Cambodia (UNTAC) a success even though a large part of the country was not under central government control, and even though the government chosen in the UN supervised elections was overthrown not long thereafter? A second question is: how can the UN ensure that 'consent' has been given in good faith and will not be withdrawn? The United Nations Angola Verification Mission (UNAVEM) is but one instance of agreements broken. A third question is: how can humanitarian relief be provided in the midst of civil war without compromising neutrality (see the United Nations Operation in Somalia, UNOSOM) and, finally: how can guarantees of 'protection' be made without compromising the commitment to use force only in self-defence (United Nations Mission in Bosnia and Herzegovina, UNMIBH)?

Many of these sticky questions seem to have arisen from an unspoken but erroneous assumption that because UN troops were well prepared and included personnel from major powers, they would not be challenged – but they were. Also, wars between nations may be suspended and construed as 'peace', but civil wars require an extended development and reconciliation process. This is because former enemies must live with each other; peace is not just a matter of respecting state borders.[3] Finally, when so many functions and the majority of clients in expanded peacekeeping are civilian and women, why do missions continue to be dominated by military men?[4]

Women's Participation in Peacekeeping: Some Data

Data for all missions active in 1993, which includes old but continuing missions like that to Jerusalem (United Nations Truce Supervision Organization, UNTSO) but which does not include newer but completed missions like the one to Namibia (United Nations Transitional Assistance Group, UNTAG), show that member states contributed less than two per cent women military personnel. Women were an even lower percentage of civilian police.[5] The largest number of military women (more than 600) served in Somalia. Three-quarters of these were from the US and they represented eight per cent of US troops. Yet women constitute about 14 per cent of the US armed forces, thus, they were under-represented in peacekeeping.[6]

The story was different for UN civilian staff. Women constituted 32 per cent of civilian staff overall. They constituted only six per cent of the 112 policy level staff, and only in the former Yugoslavia (UNPROFOR) was there more than one woman at the policy level (3 out of 20).[7] However, women constituted 30 per cent of the other professional staff of 567 and 60 per cent of the 834 members of the largely clerical general service. The field service staff of 720 was 94 per cent men. Of the locally hired staff, 20 per cent were female – with great variation by mission.[8]

Data from 1957 to 1991 show more variation than any clear trends. This suggests that leadership plays an important role in women's opportunities to participate in peacekeeping. Indeed, if the data from one mission, Namibia (where there were a large number of women, and where women were given significant responsibility) were eliminated from the database, little change would be seen over time.

In recent years the Department of Peacekeeping Operations has been relatively systematic about collecting field data on the balance in employment between men and women. Current or nearly current data from 14 active operations are available.[9] While the military in some missions remains all male, in other missions female military personnel have increased to three per cent, and some missions have increased civilian women police to three and even five per cent.[10] This includes the missions to East Timor and Kosovo, which are the first missions to have gender components. Nevertheless, interviews suggest that no great effort has been made to get member states to contribute women military personnel, while efforts have been made to increase the number of women civilian police.

In operations that are new, large and multidimensional gender balance has not improved overall for civilian staff, but women have attained higher-level posts. In Kosovo women constitute 25 per cent of the professional staff overall and 17 per cent of policy level staff. In East Timor they constitute 21 per cent of the professional staff and 16 per cent of the policy level staff.[11] In other operations women range from ten per cent to more than 30 per cent of the professional staff, but their participation at the policy level is limited.

General service staff remains largely female. UNTSO (Jerusalem) and the United Nations Mission for the Referendum in Western Sahara (MINURSO) are low exceptions with only 18 and 28 per cent women, respectively.

Field service staff continues to be largely male, but in East Timor women constitute 21 per cent of the field service staff, and in Kosovo 24 per cent. This represents a significant increase. Further, five other missions reported more than ten per cent women and three others more than 20 per cent. This may be where the largest change in women's employment has occurred.

Women constituted 30 per cent of local hires in Kosovo but only 13 per cent in East Timor. There was also wide variation in the other operations. Bosnia and Herzegovina had 53 per cent women, but the usual range was between 15 and 30 per cent.[12]

In sum, in the two new, large, and multidimensional operations that were put into place after the Beijing International Women's Conference held in 1995, women have been given more responsibility.[13] New UN principles and policies, which will be discussed below, seem to have had some effect. The change in women's participation in what had been an almost all male field service should also be recognized.

Post-Beijing Principles and Guidelines

The UN has made a formal commitment to gender equality that includes a goal of achieving a 50/50 gender (male/female) balance in all professional posts at all levels. It also includes a goal of gender mainstreaming. Gender mainstreaming refers to 'the process of assessing the implications for men and for women of any planned action, including legislation, policies or programmes in all areas and at all levels'.

Gender balance is well understood and easy to measure. Because of the existing imbalance, some men see efforts toward achieving balance as directly affecting (reducing) their opportunities. They also correctly point out that just increasing the number of women in professional positions will not necessarily increase sensitivity to gender issues. This is why understanding and implementing gender mainstreaming is important. Unfortunately, gender mainstreaming is not well understood and it is difficult to measure. Further, it is important to note that gender mainstreaming is the responsibility of both men and women, and requires analysis of the concerns and experiences of both men and women. To date mainstreaming may be devoting more attention to the needs and experiences of women. This is because men's needs are already so well integrated into most policies and programmes that they are not a matter of consciousness. At present women's needs are more likely to require explicit recognition.

In 1997, in its agreed conclusions, the Economic and Social Council provided a number of guidelines to assist in the implementation of gender balance and mainstreaming. These agreed conclusions were later endorsed by the General Assembly in its resolution 52/100 of December 1997. The fact that the UN has adopted such strong policies owes much to women's hard work in preparation for the 1995 Beijing Conference and the follow-up from that conference.

Some of the agreed conclusion's more important directives are abbreviated and paraphrased below.[14]

- An assumption of gender neutrality should not be made.
- Accountability for outcomes needs to be monitored constantly and rests at the highest levels.
- Every effort must be made to broaden women's participation at all levels of decision-making.
- Gender mainstreaming does not replace the need for targeted, women-specific policies and programmes or positive legislation, nor does it substitute for gender units or focal points.
- Directives rather than discretionary guidelines are appropriate.

- Tools for gender analysis require the disaggregation of data by sex and age.
- Mechanisms for accountability and for evaluating programmes need to be established.
- The role and capacity of gender specialists and focal points including those in the field need to be enhanced.
- Political will and the allocation of adequate and, if need be, additional human and financial resources are important for the successful translation of the concept into practice.

Units concerned with economic development and with humanitarian relief probably recognized the importance of gender mainstreaming to their work earlier than units concerned with peace, disarmament, political and security issues. Thus, there are probably lessons to be learned from the implementation of gender policies in humanitarian and development units. A position adopted by the Inter-Agency Standing Committee for the Integration of a Gender Perspective in Humanitarian Assistance on 31 May 1999 is worth noting:

> The efforts of women as mediators, their roles in trying to access communication between warring groups, and so on, are often ignored in official peace mediating initiatives. In the post-conflict phase, the emphasis on the more formal levels of establishing systems of 'governance' through political parties leaves out the role and voices of women who, at the 'informal' and community level, have much to contribute in helping define terms for peace and security.
>
> In doing so, there is a failure to comply with Article 7 of the Convention for the Elimination of All Forms of Discrimination Against Women, which falls upon states' parties to ensure that women, on equal terms with men, participate in the formulation of government policy, and in non-governmental organizations concerned with the public and political life of the country. Ignoring gender equality in emergencies is not a neutral position. It supports discrimination.

Note the Inter-Agency Committee's emphasis on the contribution women can make to the peace process and to peacebuilding even if they are not part of the formal political system. Women's organizations have been energetically advancing this position and while resolutions supporting this view have not been adopted by the Economic and Social Council, on 31 October 2000 the Security Council did adopt an 18-point resolution on women and peace and security which 'encourages' the Secretary-General to increase the participation of women at decision-making levels in conflict resolution and peace processes (see Appendix II in this collection). Extensive gender-related policies and guidelines already exist for peacekeeping operations. A note should especially be made of the Committee's emphasis on the importance of UN bodies adhering to UN principles and of the importance of considering gender even in emergencies.

The Department of Peacekeeping Operations (DPKO) often works in a crisis mode. It also works in dangerous environments. Both lead to careful if not cautious recruitment. Also, DPKO frequently has difficulty obtaining contributions of troops and/or civilian police of *either* sex from member states, and the pressure to recruit civilian staff in a short time can lead to using already known individuals and to tapping already developed candidate pools. Both these processes work against the rapid achievement of gender balance. Given these difficulties, directing energy and resources to gender balance and mainstreaming may seem a distraction and a drain on resources. However, it is worth remembering that pursuing gender balance has the potential for greatly increasing the pool of talent, and that gender mainstreaming can enhance understanding of a complex situation. It may lead to new assumptions and definitions. It may suggest different approaches to the desired end. It may reveal overlooked resources and talents. Rather than a distraction, then, the pursuit of gender equality can actually enhance a mission's chance of success.

The Three 'I's

The fact that UN policy so strongly supports gender balance and mainstreaming is important. However, to achieve gender equality goals one must bear in mind the three 'I's. The first is that *Inertia* must be overcome. Institutions tend to continue as they are. The second is that energy and resources must be given to *Implementation*, to putting policies in place. Third, once policies have been implemented, they must be *Institutionalized*. They must become routine.

As a first step towards implementation, the Lessons Learned Unit of the DPKO conducted a workshop on 'Mainstreaming a Gender Perspective in Multidimensional Peace Support Operations' in Windhoek, Namibia in May 2000 for the purpose of discussing a report by that title [prepared by this author]. That report was the basis for the 31 May 2000 'Windhoek Declaration' and for 'The Namibia Plan of Action on "Mainstreaming a Gender Perspective in Multidimensional Peace Support Operations"' (see Appendix I in this collection). The report and these two documents were later presented to the Security Council for the October discussion on women, peace and security led by the Namibian representative to the

Security Council who was able to secure the 18-point resolution discussed above.

Securing firm policies and having a plan for implementation are heartening first steps. However, every student of political science knows that implementation of new policies is not always easy, and that a variety of strategies may be needed to secure the desired effect. These include demanding and monitoring enforcement of policies, becoming candidates for policy positions, educating or, more emphatically, agitating and thus creating pressure for implementation, providing resources for the implementation of policy, and, sometimes, privately creating a model programme to serve as an example for others.

In devising a strategy the goal must always be kept in mind, in this case, gender equality. But a winning strategy does not try to do everything at once. Instead, it attempts to identify specific points where action or pressure is likely to have the most impact – often by yielding second- and third-order consequences. In a UN peacekeeping operation process there are several areas to which strategists should give particular attention.

First is the construction of the Security Council mandate, the authorization for a peacekeeping operation. The mandate shapes all mission decisions (including budgeting) and is usually narrowly constructed by implementers. This is why it is important that UN principles related to gender equality, balance and mainstreaming be enunciated in the mandate. It gives legitimacy to efforts related to gender, and, equally importantly, it serves as a constant reminder to those leading the mission that they have responsibility for gender concerns. Since the Security Council is small, the strategist's target for winning inclusion of gender language is easily identifiable and those who must be persuaded are not numerous.

Mission leadership is also of great importance.[15] This is especially true of the Special Representative of the Secretary-General (SRSG), who is in charge in the field. The selection process for an SRSG is not transparent, involves a good deal of political manoeuvring, and occurs at a very high level. Strategists need to identify, publicize and champion a pool of men and women qualified for SRSG appointments. But they should also develop a set of criteria to be applied as a measure of the gender competence of *all* candidates for SRSG. And such competence should be a prerequisite of appointment. Since these appointments are at a high level, candidates will have a public record. It should be possible to determine whether or not they have themselves had gender training, whether or not they have taken a public position on gender equality, and to determine the gender of the ten most senior staff selected by him/her while holding his/her current position.

The recruitment process as a whole merits analysis, too. In recent research it was found that those in the business of recruiting expressed regular frustration over the lack of qualified women available for employment in peacekeeping, while apparently qualified women expressed frustration over not finding a way to gain such employment. It was as though welcoming ads and announcements entered one end of a dark tunnel and expressions of interest and résumés entered the other end, and never the twain did meet. This is an area in which research and education might pay off.

Planning and budgeting begin even before the mandate is completed and, of course, continue until the mission ends. While each mission is unique, standard planning procedures also exist. This is an area in which institutionalization of gender balance and especially gender mainstreaming should be the goal. Standard checklist items need to be developed which consider the different circumstances and needs of men and women, and which raise the question of how decisions and programmes affect women and men. These items need to become routine and to be a part of all planning and budgeting. Until gender equality is more closely approximated, gender units and specialists should probably be a part of every mission.

Gender training for peacekeepers has been developed both at the UN and privately over the last several years. Several curricula are available. This is an area where the priority is implementation. Contributing member states have the responsibility for training their troops in their own countries, although the DPKO can supply materials and, on occasion, trainers for gender training. Home country training, though, tends to be uneven, and so further training is provided to troops on their arrival at an operation. The problem there is time: there are only a few days available and much to be done. Further, civilian police and civilian staff should also receive gender training; so should the large number of non-governmental organization personnel who are important to and work closely with many missions. Training, then, is an area requiring first, implementation, and second, institutionalization. Training is by definition education, but having materials available is only a first step. Materials must also be used, and then behaviour must be monitored. Monitoring of behaviour may need to be done by outsiders, but training must be done by those who command, administer or employ UN personnel. Because the norms for gender interaction are highly variable among the countries providing peacekeeping personnel and may be different in the countries to which peacekeepers are sent, it is important that UN standards be clear, understood, and adhered to. This is an area in which condoned misbehaviour can affect the legitimacy and even the success of a mission.

Finally, just as leaders should not be eligible for appointment without meeting minimum standards related to gender equality, so leaders, other administrators, and even individuals need to be held accountable for their performance in matters related to gender equality. This requires the creation of formal accountability measures, their application, and consequences for those who excel or who fail on the basis of such measurement.

Conclusion

The new, multidimensional peacekeeping missions have profound effects on women. Current UN policies and guidelines have recognized this, and fully support women's participation in peacekeeping and also support attentiveness to their needs and circumstances, that is, gender mainstreaming. The UN's commitment to gender balance and mainstreaming is clear; however, that commitment is new and implementation is far from perfect. Implementation is an immediate concern. For the most part institutionalization lies further in the future.

Supporters of gender balance and mainstreaming will have to develop a variety of strategies including education, agitation, service in policy positions and as volunteers, and creative example setting to assist in the process of overcoming inertia and resistance. Good targets for the supporters of gender equality are the creation of the mandate, the selection of senior leadership, the recruitment process, planning and budgeting, training, and the creation, application, and use of accountability measures.

Even though women's participation in conflict resolution and peace processes is now encouraged, it is likely to be difficult to achieve. Effective participation for women, their perspective, and their needs in the peacemaking and the treaty creating process has been rare. Traditionally participation in peacemaking and treaty creation has been restricted to those who have the will and capacity to resort to arms if not satisfied. Democratic theory, however, calls for participation by all who will be affected by a decision. It is particularly in small but deadly civil wars that women, some of whom have fought, and others who have refused to participate in the fighting, have begun to insist on participation in the shaping of peace. This has been particularly true of women from a variety of African countries. While women have to some degree been included in the post-peace, post-peacemaking process of peacebuilding, reconciliation and economic development, there is still a long way to go.

Because women's role in peacekeeping and peacebuilding follows the construction of peace agreements, the crucial issue may be their participation on the shaping of peace accords. There the bottom-line question is: how can the unarmed be effective participants in processes now dominated by the armed?

NOTES

1. For more details see Judith Hicks Stiehm, 'Peacekeeping and Peace Research: Men's and Women's Work', in *Women and Politics,* Vol.18, No.1, 1997, pp.27–51. Also, the UN Department of Peacekeeping Operations maintains an informative website at www.un.org/Depts/dpko.
2. The 1999 UN-sponsored elections creating an independent East Timor (then governed by Indonesia) did not have a happy result.
3. And what should a reconciliation process include? Truth commissions? War crimes trials? Shared activities? And do we fully understand the second- and third-order consequences of innovations like truth commissions and war crimes trials? And can any peace be stable without a restored economy?
4. By definition a peacekeeping operation has a military component; however, a mission does not have to be led by its military commander. To date two missions have been led by civilian women. Dame Margaret Anstee led one of the missions to Angola and Elisabeth Rehn led the mission in Bosnia-Herzegovina for a period of time.
5. UN civilian police do not police; they train and observe. This means that they must be senior and experienced officers, which makes the recruitment pool for women small.
6. Presumably this is because the US tends to send a high percentage of combat troops on peacekeeping missions, and combat restrictions are still in place for US Army women.
7. Persons classified as P-5, D-1, D-2 or ASG/USG are included as 'policy level' personnel. There are four lower levels of professional staff (P-1, P-2, P-3, and P-4); these are not considered policy makers.
8. These data are from 1993, prior to the existence of most UN policy directing gender balance and mainstreaming. They are available from several sources including the article by Stiehm (n.1 above).
9. Note that policies on gender balance and mainstreaming were in place when these data were collected.
10. The Cyprus mission reports 5 of 35 police are women.
11. Field reports presented at the Seminar on Gender Mainstreaming held in Windhoek, Nambia, 29–31 May 2000.
12. UN jobs are in demand by the local population because the pay is relatively high.
13. Gender units were also part of the planning for these operations; however full accounts of how the units have worked out in practice are not yet available.
14. A more detailed account of UN policies and guidelines appears in *Mainstreaming a Gender Perspective in Multidimensional Peace Support Operations*, a report prepared by Judith Stiehm for the Department of Peacekeeping Operations, Lessons Learned Unit, August 2000. It is available as an official UN publication.
15. See Stiehm cited above and Louise Olsson's case study of Namibia (UNTAG) in this volume.

'Women and Peace and Security': The Politics of Implementing Gender Sensitivity Norms in Peacekeeping

HENRY F. CAREY

Without international action, women caught in conflict will have no security of any kind, whatever the definition. And without women's participation, the peace process itself suffers, for there will be neither peace nor development. In your own words [Security Council Members] you have said women are half of every group and community. They are therefore not half of any form of solution. How can we in all conscience bring war lords to the peace table, but not women?

Noeleen Heyser, UNIFEM Executive Director
Security Council, 24 October 2000

Violence against women is a crime against humanity, be it in times of peace or in times of war. There are no excuses to make violence tolerable, be it physical, psychological, sexual abuse, slavery or traditional practices that violate the physical integrity of girls and women.

Harri Holkeri, General Assembly President,
on the International Day to Eliminate Violence against Women, 25 November 2000

Norms comprise the rules and goals of governing which constitute a regime type.[1] International regimes[2] regulate international politics without world government through cooperation among states. Because the international norms are less clear and more uncertain in theory and *praxis*, international regimes vary more than domestic ones (viz., democracy, authoritarianism), particularly governing war and peace. In recent years, the international humanitarian law and peacekeeping regimes have been strengthened. The UN Security Council (UNSC) expanded peace enforcement and peacekeeping and created the *ad hoc* tribunals for the former Yugoslavia and Rwanda, which have established criminal precedents against sexual violence. The proposed International Criminal Court, which is close to entering into force, along with the Tribunals' decisions, have reinforced the international regime protecting women *per se* from sexual violence. The gender mainstreaming regime incorporates the sexual violence norms, along with the rights of women to be represented by women in decision-making in UN peace missions, and goals to address the needs of women and girls in war and post-war contexts. Broad coalitions of NGOs, social movements and states have convinced UN member-states that 'women as victims of war' and 'women as creators of peace'[3] should be systematically involved in UN peace missions. While their arguments about women's more pacific nature were implicit,[4] arguments adduced in UN debates and lobbying cited women's right to political participation and their need to influence the design and implementation of peace missions directly affecting them. Women and girls are disproportionately the main civilian victims and survivors of war, and men are disproportionately represented in decision-making and implementation. Existing criminal prohibitions of violence against civilians have not protected women due to sexism, oversight and ignorance of women's needs as heads of households (with insecure land tenure and economic security) and their vulnerabilities to rape during wars. In a perfect world, special attention to women's rights and needs might not be necessary. But because we live in an imperfect world, NGOs (e.g., the Women's International League for Peace and Freedom), governments (e.g., Namibia) and UN agencies (such as UNIFEM – the UN Development Fund for Women) have lobbied for gender[5] mainstreaming norms in customary international law, treaties, soft UN resolutions and policies.

The epitome of the new regime is the unanimously passed UNSC Resolution 1325 (31 October 2000). It legally requires gender mainstreaming on all UN peacekeeping and related state actions. Forty-three states, as diverse as China, the US, Bangladesh, the United Arab Emirates, Nepal, Malawi, and Argentina, testified in favour of the new gender security norms. We might name this new regime either 'women and peace and security', the title of the UNSC hearings before Resolution 1325, or simply the former mantra of 'gender mainstreaming'.

A more specific international regime, 'gender mainstreaming in peace missions', applies these principles of women's rights[6] and humanitarian needs to the formulation and implementation of UN peacemaking and peacekeeping missions. The roots of this regime begin with the Charter's Preamble listing women's rights as a goal. Soon after, the Sub-Commission on Women was established to promote women's rights. The women's summits and General Assembly extraordinary sessions since 1975 encouraged new women's networks and norms. The first UN Decade on

Women from 1975 fostered the 1981 Convention on the Elimination of All Forms of Discrimination Against Women (CEDAW). At the 1993 Vienna World Conference on Human Rights, women's NGOs argued that violence against women, '[as a] global wrong, requires a worldwide solution'[7] integrating gender into human rights protection. The 1995 Beijing Women's Platform for Action set an initial goal of 30 per cent female representation in UN decision-making, a goal also adopted by the Committee of the Women's Convention. The 1998 statute of the International Criminal Court mandated gender balance among judges and prosecutors[8] and considered rape a grave breach of international humanitarian law, both norms established by the *ad hoc* criminal tribunals for Rwanda and the former Yugoslavia.

New norms and institutions emerged rapidly in 2000. The UNSC recognized women as actors in the peace process on International Women's Day, 8 March 2000, and in April they considered the situation facing Afghani women. In March, the Human Rights Committee[9] required states to document measures to prevent unwanted pregnancies, clandestine abortions, female infanticide, burning of widows, dowry killings and female genital mutilation, and prohibited regulating clothing in public or confinement within houses.[10] Its General Comment No.28 on Equality of Rights between Men and Women warned against pre-natal sex selection and abortion of female foetuses. Another treaty-based committee, on the Elimination of Racial Discrimination, issued General Recommendation XXV that it would consider the interrelationship between gender and racial discrimination in its review of states' reports.[11]

The UN High Commissioner for Human Rights issued a gender mainstreaming policy statement,[12] and held technical assistance missions and a May 1999 workshop for UN rapporteurs and chairs of human rights committees.[13] In May, on the tenth anniversary of the UN Mission in Namibia, the Lessons Learned Unit of the UN Department of Peacekeeping Operations issued the 'Windhoek Declaration and Namibian Plan of Action on Mainstreaming a Gender Perspective in Multidimensional Peace Support Operations'.[14] UNSC Statement 6816 acknowledged that 'peace is inextricably linked with equality between men and women'.[15] The General Assembly's 23rd special session from 5 to 10 June on 'Women 2000: Gender Equality, Development and Peace' reviewed progress since the 1995 Beijing, 4th World Conference on Women. Its final document called for:

- zero-tolerance campaigns for violence against women;
- laws and other measures to address negative traditional practices, including honour-crimes and dowry-related violence;

- mainstreaming a gender perspective into national immigration policies by recognizing gender persecution as grounds for asylum; and
- proper policies to respond to the disproportionate impacts of AIDS and other sexually transmitted diseases on women and girls.[16]

Secretary-General Kofi Annan designated the highest-ranking woman at the UN, Deputy Secretary-General Louise Fréchette, to oversee the plan to implement the recommendations of the 23 August 'Brahimi Report', prepared for the Millennium Summit of 150 heads of state, on how to improve UN peacekeeping. In her address to participants in the World March of Women on 17 October 2000 at UN Headquarters, Fréchette showed her sensitivity by focusing on female poverty:

> Poverty has a gender, and it is feminine. Yet, the majority of poor women are gainfully employed ... If we work together and combine our efforts, the twenty-first century will see rapid progress in the fight to end poverty and violence against women. Your campaign has helped raise consciousness about the many obstacles which still prevent women from fully enjoying their rights.[17]

The landmark UNSC Resolution 1325 came a week after the UNSC held unusual, open hearings on 24–25 October on the 55th anniversary of the UN's founding, preceded by a one-day closed session on 23 October. Female experts from Somalia, Zambia and Guatemala testified under the Arria formula of parliamentary procedure. The absence of consensus meant that representatives from the two existing gender units in East Timor and Kosovo could not be invited. Luz Mendez of the National Union of Guatemalan Women described the first peace treaty with terms on gender sensitivity.[18] In the subsequent open sessions, all 43 states advocated increased sensitivity towards gender in peacekeeping and women's NGO participation. The path-breaking discussion was laudatory and vague, except when the United Arab Emirates criticized Israel's treatment of Palestinian women.[19] Britain and Canada presented a new human rights training manual for peacekeepers, which women's NGOs found exemplary in treating gender concerns.

Resolution 1325 has 18 points mandating gender mainstreaming in all UN activities, especially peacekeeping, including:

- for states to increase women's representation in conflict resolution and reconstruction to account for their needs, to support local women's peace initiatives, and to respect their human rights, particularly involving elections, police and the judiciary;
- for the Secretary-General to implement his plan to increase female

participation[20] as special representatives, in field-based, human rights and humanitarian operations, and among civilian, police and military observers, and to include gender units and involve women's NGOs in all peace processes; and to study the impact of armed conflict on women and girls;[21] and

- for all parties to protect women and girls from sexual violence and to prosecute those responsible.

The Resolution did not include an ambitious US recommendation for UNSC monitoring by 'establishing a very specifically mandated, expert panel or working group to report on mechanisms that will ensure equal representation of women in peacekeeping and peace-building operations'.[22]

Mainstreaming Peacekeeping

While large variations exist across cultures with respect to women, no culture sanctions violence against women. UN member-states are able to support the new regime in principle, even if practice will not change automatically. Already, universal human rights and humanitarian law institutions prohibit sexual violence and protect women's rights. What is new is the legal requirement to include women in decision-making and implementation in peace missions. Both treaty-based and UN Charter-based human rights institutions have quickly adopted and begun implementing gender equality and mainstreaming norms. As with human rights generally, states are better at proclaiming their commitments than in protecting them. Implementing gender mainstreaming norms depends partly on existing and imperfect mechanisms of human and women's rights protection and UN peacemaking and peacekeeping, and untested gender mainstreaming processes.

The most comprehensive study, *Mainstreaming a Gender Perspective in Multidimensional Peace Operations*, was reviewed by the seminar preceding the Windhoek Declaration. The case studies, upon which the general study is based, has not, at the time of writing, been released. According to Angela King, the Secretary-General's special gender issues adviser, it concluded from UN peacekeeping in Bosnia, Cambodia, El Salvador, Namibia and South Africa that:

- local women confide more in female peacekeepers;
- women negotiators understand and articulate the implications of peace processes for women better than do men;

- peace missions with high percentages of women, such as Namibia (40 per cent women) and South Africa (50 per cent), have been successful; and
- if at least 30 per cent of mission personnel are female, then local women more quickly join peace committees, which are less hierarchical and more responsive to female concerns.[23]

These plausible conclusions reflect consensus within the UN bureaucracy and among interested member-states, but also ignore divisive issues. The same holds for the updated Graça Machel report on armed conflict and children, which includes 'women in peace-building' as one of its five topics.[24]

High rates of female participation have not been maintained since the electoral verification mission that decolonized Namibia in late 1989, when most staff were permanent UN employees. Female percentages have decreased, as missions and outside staff have increased. Beginning with the International Civilian Mission to Haiti (MICIVIH) in 1993, human rights generalists in missions have monitored gender issues, such as state-sponsored rape.

Since spring 2000, gender specialists have been used in 'gender focal points' – in the human rights unit of Western Sahara, in the second UN Mission in Sierra Leone, in 12 of the 13 districts in East Timor and in five regional offices covering 30 municipalities in Kosovo. At about the same time, gender units of five or six people were established in Kosovo and East Timor. Both focal points and units have developed codes of conduct for military and civilian personnel on gender awareness and women's rights. Unfortunately, none of the women's NGOs in Freetown had even heard of the focal point person, who had not asked any of them to document human rights violations. Isha Dyfan testified in the UNSC closed session on 23 October that:

> The Operation in Sierra Leone has a gender point person in the human rights verification unit, designated to systematically monitor and report on violations against women. This element of UNAMSIL is a model that is carving new ground. We hope it will be routinely applied in peace support operations, but there are lessons to be learned. The Brahimi Report emphasizes the need for Peace Support Operations to engage with local groups – it seems this particular unit in Sierra Leone [is] yet to engage its constituency.[25]

In the second intervention in the open UNSC session on 24 October, Angela King noted that a collaborative, three-year study, *Mainstreaming a Gender Perspective in Multidimensional Peace Operations*,[26] had concluded: 'that the most important lesson learned is that lessons are not always learned. Lessons from Namibia and South Africa had little effect on Cambodia or Bosnia Herzegovina, for example. Gender equality issues are absolutely essential to the success of any peace operation.'[27]

In addition to peacekeeping, the UNSC sanctioned gender integration in three UN-mediated peacemaking processes. The UN transitional mission in South Africa, along with various NGOs, encouraged the mostly male, constitutional negotiators to adopt principles from the Convention on the Elimination of Discrimination Against Women (CEDAW) and the Beijing Platform for Action. Female activists from trade unions, the African National Congress and Anglican Church groups pushed part of this agenda into the new constitution. A conflict arose between proponents of gender equality and African customary law permitting gender discrimination, which had been curtailed under laws inherited from British and Dutch colonialism. The constitution permits some customary law prerogatives of chiefs to distribute property. By permitting women to become chiefs and banning discrimination, the constitution attempts to reconcile discrepancies, though many legal interpretations remain for South Africa's courts and legislature.[28]

In 1996 in Guatemala, female participation in peace talks produced the Office for the Defence of Indigenous Women's Rights.[29] Its effectiveness, according to the Secretary-General, 'could be undermined if it does not receive strong government support in carrying out its mandate'.[30] Though the government pledged to protect everyone, on 30 July 1998 men with grenades, machetes and firearms assaulted 30 members of *Mama Maquin*, a women's NGO defending rights of returning refugee and displaced women.[31]

In Burundi, UNIFEM and the Nyerere Fund financed two expert missions to consult with representatives from 19 negotiating parties, who met from 17 to 20 July 2000 at an all-women's peace conference in Arusha.[32] Previously, only two out of 126 delegates at the negotiations had been women.[33] The negotiations' facilitator, Nelson Mandela, accepted 23 of the conference's recommendations, including female rights to inherit land and to educational equality.

Secretary-General Annan has emphasized gender mainstreaming, including at the 24 October 2000 UNSC session. He reports annually, through the Commission on the Status of Women and ECOSOC, on progress on implementing the Beijing Platform for Action's 12 areas.[34] In the year following the Sub-Commission's Resolution 1999/15, he failed to provide information on women and the right to development, but promised to provide it in his report on the Right to Development for the 2001 General Assembly session.[35]

For Charter-based bodies, on 20 October 2000, the Third Committee passed a draft resolution for the Assembly's consideration, which urged the Secretary-General to appoint more women as special representatives and envoys in peacekeeping, peacebuilding, preventive diplomacy, and economic and social development.[36] None of the current 61 Special Representatives of the Secretary-General (SRSGs) are women.[37] The UNDP *Human Development Report* for 2000 contains many indices on gender development that affect each country's 'human development rating'. For the 52nd Sub-Commission session, High Commissioner for Human Rights Mary Robinson submitted a report on 'Systematic Rape, Sexual Slavery and Slavery-Like Practices during Armed Conflicts'.[38] The UN Human Rights Commission's Special Rapporteur on Violence Against Women and Its Causes and Consequences, Radhika Coomaraswamy (of Sri Lanka), represents the epitome of UN monitoring of women as victims. Originally, women's NGOs argued that her office should also examine discrimination. Since its full title includes 'causes and consequences', she has begun to examine social-economic policies, inequality and violence against women.

ECOSOC Resolution 1996/31 is on Integration of the Human Rights of Women and the Gender Perspective: Violence against Women and the creation of the UN Division on the Promotion of Women. ECOSOC Resolution 1997/2 called for gender mainstreaming in all UN policies and programmes. The Spring 2000 Annual Meeting of the Human Rights Commission considered 'Integration of the Human Rights of Women and the Gender Perspective' as an agenda item, with the sub-topic of 'Violence Against Women'.[39] The Human Rights Commission Resolution 1998/51 calls for 'Integrating the Human Rights of Women throughout the United Nations System'. The September 2000 Millennium Summit of 150 heads of state committed itself to promoting gender equality and female empowerment to stimulate development.

For treaty-based bodies, 35 states intend to sign two recently concluded protocols to the Convention on the Rights of the Child relating to child prostitution and trafficking.[40] Sixty-two states have signed the Women's Convention Protocol since its 10 December 1999 introduction on the anniversary of the Universal Declaration of Human Rights. Italy became the tenth state to ratify on 22 September 2000, enabling the Protocol to enter into force on 22 December 2000. It unfortunately contains an 'opt-out' clause permitting states to withdraw, though Article 17 permits no reservations.[41] The General Assembly's June 2000 Review of the Fourth World Conference described the Optional Protocol as:

> one of the greatest legislative achievements in the area of the human rights of women since the Fourth World Conference on Women – and

> the Rome Statute of the International Criminal Court, which provides that rape, sexual slavery, enforced prostitution, forced pregnancy, enforced sterilization and other forms of sexual violence are war crimes when committed in the context of armed conflict and also, under defined circumstances, crimes against humanity.[42]

In civil society, finally, the International Committee of the Red Cross is formulating guidelines to protect and assist women and girls in armed conflict and developing clearer norms prohibiting sexual violence in war.[43]

Successes and Challenges to Gender Mainstreaming in Peacekeeping

Institutional responses and learning on gender mainstreaming developed slowly in the 1990s. Approaches were *ad hoc* and isolated. As peacekeeping operations faltered, gender issues were erroneously considered peripheral or ignored. The joint UN/OAS human rights monitoring mission (MICIVIH) in Haiti, possibly the first to monitor gender rights, operated from 1993 until it was ordered by the coup government to withdraw in July 1994 but was then restored after the September 1994 US/UN invasion under UNSC Resolution 940.[44] A peacekeeping mission of decreasing complexity over time operated until late 1999. (The OAS remained until after the May 2000 Senate electoral fraud.) MICIVIH documented the rape-terror campaign from 1993 to 1994 committed by the Haitian paramilitary group FRAPH. MICIVIH reported 66 cases of politically motivated rape between January and May 1994.[45] Fifty-two per cent of rape victims surveyed at its clinic were related to anti-regime activists; 18 per cent were activists themselves.[46] MICIVIH's monitoring and humanitarian assistance have ensured that rape is no longer a taboo subject in Haiti.

Almost no Haitian trials for rape have occurred. The only prosecutions have been the October 2000 convictions of 50 former army officers for the massacre of peasants and fishermen at Rabateau, the 1995 conviction *in absentia* of coup leader Michel François, and a late 2000 trial for the Carrefour massacre of seven youths. Compared to the comprehensive 1993 Truth Commission report on El Salvador, the UNSC gave little support or publicity to Haiti's 1994 truth commission, *La Commission Nationale de Vérité et Justice*. It concluded that the increase in rapes between 1991and 1994 resulted from generalized repression. Lacking UNSC support, the Haitian government has not followed *Vérité et Justice*'s recommendations to facilitate prosecutions; investigate named rapists; legislate a clear and expanded definition of rape; protect victims during trials; educate those treating victims; establish a female police unit for investigating gender crimes; increase the number of shelters for battered or abused women; and legislate to decriminalize abortion and adultery.[47] To be fair, Haiti had no functioning legislature from 1996 to 2000.[48]

In the peacekeeping phase, women's NGOs like Solidarity of Haitian Women (SOFA), *Konbit Fanm Saj* (Wise Women's Group), and *Kay Fanm* (House of Women), have monitored human and women's rights and assisted gender abuse victims. *Kay Fanm* started the only safe-house for women. Assisting victims of sexual violence is complicated by the taboo on discussing rape; the common practice of *plasaj*, when unmarried men and women live together; men who live part time with two or more women; and/or women who have more than one man coming to see them. From 1998 to 1999, Miriam Merlet led a loose coalition of previously politically polarized, women's NGOs to negotiate in critical engagement with the parliament, which is composed almost entirely of men.[49]

The first gender units were established by the UN Department of Peacekeeping Operations, first in Kosovo in June 1999 and then in East Timor in October. Both mandates aspired to create sustainable gender development and thus development itself. The Office of Gender Affairs (OGA) in the UN peacekeeping Mission in Kosovo (UNMIK), headed by Fatima Almana, sought to develop:

> economic, health, legal and other information pertinent to assisting women to participate with men equally in planning and decision-making; including women and women's NGOs in all sectors of the new civil administration; to target apt humanitarian assistance to widows, female heads of households and victims of sexual violence; training police and judicial officials on women's rights and forensic investigation of sexual and domestic violence; to generate and analyse statistical indicators and other documentation on specific female problems and gender mainstreaming efforts in both UNMIK and in Kosovo; and to assist UNMIK's SRSG and the investigations of gender-related crimes by the International Criminal Tribunal for Yugoslavia.[50]

This extensive list of duties, according to Suvira Chaturvedi, Chief Technical Advisor of UNIFEM's Priština, Kosovo office, meant that:

> Much work… [needed] to be done in mainstreaming gender perspectives in Kosovo's economic recovery and development. The situation of women and their expressed needs and potential require greater and equal attention. The issue is related to the lack of conceptual clarity on gender, limited technical expertise and

> application of gender-sensitive approaches in practice. These were also some of the findings of a Participatory Evaluation that took place this month [October 2000] and involved local and international organizations.[51]

Kosovo has had difficulty prosecuting rape. Anne Garrels reported in 2000 that Kosovo's reluctance to prosecute rape follows similar cultural patterns as in Haiti:

> Terrified women, victims of domestic violence and rape, sit in the lobby of Priština's Center for the Protection of Women and Children. Saldia Ahmedi, who founded this office, says that they have nowhere else to turn because the police do not move fast enough and the courts offer no witness protection. She has repeatedly asked the United Nations to improve training: 'We are asking the UN to do especially training for gender-based violence for all uniformed persons.' And when cases do come to trial, the OSCE reports that judges harass victims.[52]

UNIFEM's three projects in Kosovo complement UNMIK. UNIFEM financed training of women for elections and governing during workshops held in Kosovo's five regions from March to the 28 October 2000 local elections. UNIFEM sought the Beijing Platform's goal of 30 per cent female participation among candidates. The training of 600 women as candidates was conducted by the Organization of Security and Cooperation in Europe, the National Democratic Initiative, Concern (an Irish NGO), and the Star Network (a US NGO). It included civic education, party training and election monitoring. UNIFEM plans to train the newly elected, local office holders and prepare female candidates for Kosovo's provincial elections in 2001.

Because UNMIK and the Food and Agriculture Organization do not target women, UNIFEM has financed a US$50,000 pilot project to train women of all ethnicities for agriculture in Podujevo. World Vision International provided agricultural tools including tractors and seeds. UNIFEM financed the training of 16 women to use tractors and 200 women in agribusiness. UNIFEM established a gender mainstreaming task force in September 1999 that informs UNMIK staff on developments on women in government, business, political participation and as victims. After meeting with the UNIFEM task force, UNMIK Director Bernard Kouchner directed all UN agencies to track trafficking in women.

The East Timor peacekeeping mission (UNTAET) originally had no plans for gender officers.[53] Then, two mid-level, gender focal points were assigned to the human rights and governance offices. Only the latter was created, and upgraded to an OGA in spring 2000. Director Sherrill Whittington expanded its staff to six women, with two more local Timorese to be hired. She noted that OGA's role was subservient to UNTAET's main objective to provide security and maintain law and order throughout East Timor and establish effective administration.[54] Whittington would have preferred to follow the UNMIK model with OGA reporting to the SRSG, which 'would have provided a rare opportunity for peacekeeping missions to design public institutions which mainstream a gender-based rights approach in institutional and human resource planning, policies and programming'.[55] Instead, the OGA for East Timor reports to the Deputy SRSG for Governance and Public Administration, which works closely with the National Planning and Development Agency, one of four branches of East Timor's transitional government. Aside from this direct access, the OGA established a gender task force, rather than following UNMIK's reliance on UNIFEM. It trains and oversees the UNTAET gender focal points. From 14 to 17 June 2000 the OGA convened Timorese delegates to establish the East Timorese Women's Platform for Action. Its goals include:

> participation in decision making; the establishment of a gender-sensitive legal and justice system with compensation and reparations for women victims of violence experienced in the last 24 years of Indonesian military occupation; the development of an inclusive Constitution; a special focus on vulnerable groups; and literacy programmes for women and girls.[56]

In its first six months, the OGA held workshops on gender mainstreaming for UNTAET staff; developed guidelines and working relationships with UNTAET units including CIVPOL police; facilitated access of women's NGOs to UNTAET; and generated statistics and papers on issues, especially education and returning refugees. The UN Development Programme increased from four gender indicators to evaluating gender performance in all UN reporting categories.

UNIFEM with UNTAET have assessed the 'Leadership Development (of women) in Peace Building' and developed a strategy to encourage women's representation on public bodies. As in Kosovo, they will train women as voters, candidates and NGO monitors for the 2001 elections. UNIFEM collaborated with Australia's UNIFEM national committee to provide trauma counselling for women affected by atrocities.[57]

Negative Signals on Gender Mainstreaming

Despite rapid progress, gender mainstreaming has not realized its potential. The 'Brahimi Report' did not even mention the word 'women'. Its ten-person panel had only two women members.[58] The Secretary-General's 2000 annual report does not mention women.[59] While he did report in the previous year that women's status in the Secretariat has improved since 1970,[60] many complaints and lawsuits allege sex discrimination. When states submitted reports to the 2000 Beijing+5 conference, many Muslim (Jordan, United Arab Emirates, Sudan) and African states (Kenya, Zimbabwe, Burundi, Rwanda and South Africa) asserted that they do not discriminate against women, but do have customary personal laws and constitutional pluralism clauses. The latter prevent women from living on land owned by their late husbands.[61]

Generally, the UN does not consider itself bound by international treaties – including anti-discrimination conventions. It is argued that treaties apply only to states; international civil servants are exempt from state jurisdictions; and peacekeeping forces are gathered as 'coalitions of the willing' under separate national commands. Basing his argument on a Joint Inspection Unit report, the Secretary-General notes that:

> The (human rights) instruments…are applicable only to the States that have ratified them and not to any intergovernmental organizations to which those States might belong. If States wish to make the provisions or the principles of such instruments applicable to an international organization, they can do so by means of appropriate resolutions in the organization.[62]

This appears to contradict the Secretary-General's commitments to mainstreaming.

Furthermore, states may prove lukewarm about the issue if their human rights implementation is anything to go by. UNIFEM's June 2000 report, *Progress of the World's Women*, concludes that only six countries out of 183 have met the criteria in 12 critical areas of the 1995 Beijing Platform for Action.[63] Many of the 166 states that have ratified the Women's Convention have specified reservations such as by Muslim states, along with Thailand, Brazil, Korea, Tunisia and New Zealand, which undermine its aims. Pakistan, for example, reserves its constitution's superiority over any convention provision.[64] States are required to submit reports to the Committee on the Elimination of Discrimination Against Women (CEDAW) every four years on their compliance with the Convention's provisions. Two hundred country reports have never been filed. Some, like Haiti, have not submitted four overdue periodic reports. Another 49 have been submitted too late for follow-up hearings. Only a dozen countries have submitted their reports on time.[65] The United States has never ratified the Women's Convention.

Some women's rights protection has *worsened*. Peacekeepers guilty of sexual violence and other war crimes in Bosnia, Haiti, Somalia, Sierra Leone, Liberia and Kosovo have had immunity in their home countries and abroad because they helped to stop wars. It may be difficult to stop peacekeepers' (humanitarian law) violations, but no military necessity excuses their rapes, tit-for-tat extra-judicial executions, or abandoning babies resulting from consensual sex (as was noted in the closed UNSC session of 23 October 2000 because irate mothers had raised their 'ECOMOG babies' at Nigerian peacekeeping troops departing from Sierra Leone). The West was uninterested in prosecuting Nigerians because they were willing to fight against the Revolutionary United Front – though the crimes may have led the rebels to break the peace accord in May 2000 and take hundreds of peacekeeping troops hostage. Most crimes committed by UN peacekeepers have not been condemned by UN human rights bodies. The Secretariat has been negotiating criminal courts for Sierra Leone and Cambodia. An agreement between the Sierra Leone government and the UN would have given a Special Court[66] fewer powers than the *ad hoc* tribunals for Yugoslavia and Rwanda – this for a country where more than half the women and adolescent girls were reportedly raped and two million refugees fled rebel atrocities. It would not be able to request the surrender of fugitives or assert primacy over Sierra Leone or foreign courts. The United States did, exceptionally, prosecute a soldier in a US military court for raping and murdering a minor in Kosovo. Generally, KFOR military personnel, including local recruits, are immune from local arrest or prosecution.[67]

Most states show little interest in prosecuting rape or sexual torture cases in Afghanistan, Sri Lanka, Mexico, Peru and Turkey.[68] States resist mediation too. Russia agreed that an investigation by the Special Rapporteur on Violence against Women 'is not excluded' though security considerations prevent an invitation to carry out such an investigation.[69]

Looking to the Future

Academics raise concerns about defining and applying mainstreaming. Hilary Charlesworth argues that the terms of gender mainstreaming should be deconstructed for sexist bias:

> The United Nations … has responded to criticism of *its* marginalization of women by instituting policies of 'gender mainstreaming'... The conceptual limitation is that *gender* is assumed to be a synonym for *women*. This assumption leaves male identities unexamined and requires women to change but not men.

> Interpretations of the mandate vary; the process of implementing 'gender policy' can become radically simplified to the point of irrelevance and inconvenience. In these ways, both sex and gender can be stripped of their radical potential.[70]

The 'women and peace and security' regime has established clear norms in principles and a few implementation imperatives, such as enforcing laws on sexual violence and permitting minimal women's participation in decision-making. Much discretion remains about how to implement mainstreaming in different peacemaking and peacekeeping contexts. This vagueness results from the regime's large aspirational scope and its short track record. Any new international regime, such as the new OSCE and OAS treaties banning bribery or the CEDAW Optional Protocol, is a long way from institutionalization.[71] Norms represent only a first step, a necessary but not sufficient condition to end impunity for sexual violence and promote gender equality and responsiveness during the long night of war and the painful day of building peace. States supported Resolution 1325 as much to support unobjectionable principles without concrete commitments requiring sacrifices as from genuine desires to address concerns of war-torn women and families. Over time, some of these aspirations will become norms and embedded in standard operating procedures; others will prove a dead letter. Other implementation issues will remain 'work in progress'. We shall discover whether women decision-makers, assuming they are afforded opportunities, are more likely to opt for persuasion over coercion than their male counterparts and whether, as we tend to assume, women are more able to address female concerns in war and post-war situations. UN bodies and states are unlikely, except perhaps in countries that observe Shar'ia law, to oppose gender mainstreaming on principle, but they may ignore them under the exigencies of the moment or the budgetary constraints of the day.

High initial support for gender mainstreaming thus reflects what political scientists call 'valence issues' on which most agree in principle. Mainstreaming may resemble divisive 'position issues' over implementation options, thereby overshadowing any early, exciting successes from female participation, as the policy competes for scarce resources and faces structural constraints. In Kosovo, for example, complaints of insufficient peacekeepers and a biased judiciary may take priority, even under conditions of relative peace. When peace breaks down, as in Somalia in 1993 or in Sierra Leone in 2000, mainstreaming is ever needed but competes for attention. Attempting to resolve general issues could benefit women but might thereby reduce the demand for mainstreaming.

Two gender affairs offices and two dozen focal points can only reform peacekeeping if they can persuade senior decision-makers not to perceive mainstreaming as a competitor for other projects and resources. Proponents also need to decide whether to undertake the huge list of projects, such as that of the UNMIK OGA, or fewer projects with greater likelihood of efficacy. Many questions remain open for peace support missions: should mainstreaming be a staff (advisory) or line (functional) responsibility, or both; between whom should liaison occur; what community groups might be established; what types of gender offices in local government should be encouraged, if any; to whom will resources be allocated; how much outside involvement in local decision-making is desirable given varying commitments to gender equality; and what happens if community groups veto mission decisions? Differences of opinion exist within societies over whether to adopt affirmative action or quotas, how to protect women's property and child custody rights, and how to prioritize competing needs.

Aside from learning how to implement incipient norms, others beg for formal recognition, including:

- recognition of sexual violence as *jus cogens* crimes, which cannot be amnestied[72] and can be prosecuted anywhere, and prohibition of violent traditional practices like female genital mutilation;[73]
- equal gender rights, even in countries with traditional customary law, to inheritance of family property; custody of children; access to credit, natural resources, for court testimony and so on;
- prohibition of forced or parental-sanctioned prostitution or trafficking as a crime against humanity;
- mandatory trauma training and services to rehabilitate victims of sexual violence; and
- reparations to female survivors of universal crimes and assistance to document litigation; defendants to include not only individuals, but also corporations and states.

To date, the contribution of women's NGOs, most states and the UN towards realizing this belated, but welcome, regime represents an important juncture in world history. It needs to be demonstrated that new goals, rules and assignments are not irreconcilable with existing state interests and other international regimes. This will require constant effort and vigilance, given scarce resources, to ensure mutually satisfactory solutions. NGOs carry a particular responsibility to monitor and promote these revolutionary changes in state and UN behaviour. No matter how difficult are these challenges, the consequences are too vital not to invest all available resources and reasonable effort to succeed.

NOTES

1. Robert Keohane and Joseph Nye, *Power and Interdependence*, Boston: Little, Brown, 1977, p.19.
2. Regime 'implies not only norms and expectations that facilitate cooperation, but a form of cooperation that is more than the following of short-run self-interest'. Robert Jervis, 'Security Regimes', in Stephen D. Krasner (ed.), *International Regimes*, Ithaca: Cornell University Press, 1982, p.173.
3. Margaret Keck and Katherine Sikkink, *Activists Beyond Borders: Advocacy Networks and International Politics*, Ithaca: Cornell University Press, 1998.
4. Heads of government like Margaret Thatcher, Indira Ghandi, Golda Meir, Benazir Bhutto, and the world's first female Prime Minister Sirimavo Bandaranaike of Sri Lanka and her most recent successor Chandrika Bandaranaike Kumaratunga, or the US ambassadors to the UN, Jeanne Kirkpatrick and Madeleine Albright, all show that women leaders are not unlikely to be militaristic. Women will assume combat roles in the German armed forces, which will test female tendencies towards militarism or gender mainstreaming, or both.
5. While the term 'gender' could also refer to men, I use this term to refer only to women and girls. Claudia Card argues that 'the social meaning of "female" needs to be changed so that it no longer connotes "victim"'. See 'Rape as a Weapon of War', *Hypatia,* Vol.11, No.4, Fall 1996, p.12.
6. Given space limitations, this essay does not analyse how the protection of human rights protects women. The legal rights of women, *as such*, are found in the UN Charter (Preamble, Articles 1, 2), the Convention on the Elimination of all Forms of Discrimination against Women, the Convention on Nationality of Married Women, the International Covenant on Civil and Political Rights, the Supplementary Convention on the Abolition of Slavery, and Convention No.156 of the International Labour Organization on the Slave Trade and Institutions and Practices Similar to Slavery.
7. Berta Hernandez, Presentation, International Law Weekend, New York, November 1998.
8. Some states objected that requiring gender balance produces a 'first world bias' in tribunals because of its greater number of qualified women lawyers and judges.
9. Of the International Covenant on Civil and Political Rights.
10. UN Document CCPR/C/21/Add.10, pp.3–5, at paras 10–14.
11. UN Document A/55/18, Annex V, at paras 3–4.
12. *Human Rights*, UN High Commissioner for Human Rights, Spring 2000, pp.6–7. See reports on women and peacekeeping in the UN missions in El Salvador, Guatemala, Bosnia and Herzegovina, and the Palestinian territory including Jerusalem, pp.28–33 and UN Document, Supplement No.36 (A/55/36), Chapter VI, pp.8–10.
13. UN Document E/CN.4/2000/INFORMAL/3.
14. www.unifem.undp.org/unseccouncil/windhoek.html. The Declaration covers peace negotiations, mandates, leadership, planning, structure and resources of missions, recruitment, training, procedures, monitoring, evaluation and accountability, and public awareness.
15. www.unifem.undp.org/unseccouncil/unscngost.html.
16. General Assembly Supplement No.36 (A/55/36), Chapter VI, p.9.
17. UN Press Release DSG/SM/108/Rev.1*, 17 Oct. 2000.
18. Others included Inonge Mbikusita-Lewanika of the OAU African Women's Committee on Peace and Democracy; Isha Dyfan of the Women's International League for Peace and Freedom in Sierra Leone and New York; Faiza Jama Mohammed, a Somalian, from the Kenya Office of Equality Now; and Eugenia Piza-Lopez of International Alert in the UK. Sponsoring NGOs included Amnesty International, the Women's Commission for Refugee Women and Children, and The Hague Appeal for Peace.
19. UN Documents S/PV.4208, S/PV.4208 (Resumption 1), S/PV.4208, S/PV.4208 (Resumption 2), and S/PV.4208 (Resumption 3).
20. UN Document A/49/587.

21. UNIFEM's desired output from Resolution 1325 was to commission a study like the Graça Machel report, 'The Impact of Armed Conflict on Children' (August 1996), according to spokesperson Micol Zarb, Interview, 26 Oct. 2000.
22. Nancy Soderberg, USUN Press Release No.16 (2000). The UNSC has working groups, one of which judges Iraq's proposed oil-for-food purchases. Groups of UNSC members (and the Secretary-General) visited missions and gender specialists in Sierra Leone and East Timor.
23. Presumably, King means 'all other things being equal'. More female peacekeepers would probably not have reduced violence in Srebrenica, Tuzla, Rwanda, or Somalia.
24. She presented her updated report at the International Conference on War-Affected Children, Winnipeg, Canada, 17 September 2000, www.unifem.undp.org/machelrep.htm.
25. Copy of speech provided to the author.
26. Other studies include *Women and Post-Conflict Reconstruction*, a UNRISD funded study; Louise Olsson, *Gendering UN Peacekeeping*, Report No.53, Department of Peace and Conflict Research, Uppsala University, Sweden, including its bibliography, pp.38–43; and bibliography at www.womenwagingpeace.org.
27. UN Document S/PV.4208, 24 Oct. 2000, p.6.
28. Penelope Andrews, Presentation, Annual Meeting of the American Society for International Law, Washington, April 2000.
29. This office was praised by UN General Assembly Resolution 54/1999, para.3.
30. UN Document A/55/175, p.7, at para.32, 26 July 2000. UN Document A/55/389, p.4, 14 Sept. 2000, reports 'a qualitative deterioration of the human rights situation…[and] shortcomings in the Judiciary lead to a significant number of due process violations.
31. The Office for the Defence of Women in the Office of the Attorney General for Human Rights and the Unit for Women of the Prosecutor General's Office were reportedly investigating the attacks. UN Document E/CN.4/1999/68/Add.1, p.4, at paras 4–6.
32. UN Document A/55/271.
33. Press Release, NGO Working Group on Women and International Peace and Security, 17 October 2000. See Barbara Crossette, 'Women Seek Louder Voice as World Peacemakers', *The New York Times*, 28 May 2000, p.4.
34. UN Document E/CN.6/2000/2, 31 Dec. 1999, pp.6–8, paras 19–28. Three annual reports of the Secretary-General go to the Commission on the Status of Women on Secretariat efforts to mainstream gender and follow-up by NGOs; to ECOSOC on its coordinating function; and to the General Assembly on responses by states and NGOs to UN bodies.
35. UN Document E/CN.4/Sub.2/2000/19, 6 June 2000.
36. UN Press Release GA/SHC/3600, 20 Oct. 2000.
37. UN Document S/PV.4208 at p.8. There is only one woman out of 15 on the UNSC and only ten out of 189 Permanent Representatives. Six are the Deputy Secretary-General, the heads of UNIFEM, UNICEF, World Food Programme, World Health Organization, Assistant Secretary-General for Gender Affairs, and both High Commissioners.
38. UN Document E/CN.4/Sub.2/2000/20.
39. Recent sessions on 'Violence against Women' summarized in UN Documents E/CN.4/2000/66, 67, 68 and Add.1 to 5, E/CN.4/2000/118-E/CN.4/2000/56, E/CN.4/2000/NGO/65, 87, 119, E/CN.6/2000/6, E/CN.4/Sub.2/1999/14, and E/CN.4/2000/ NGO/56.
40. UN Document GA/9741-PI/1268.
41. Andrew Byrnes and Jane Connors, 'Enforcing the Human Rights of Women: A Complaints Procedure for the Women's Convention?', *Brooklyn Journal of International Law*, Vol.1, No.3, 1996, pp.679–783.
42. UN Document A/55/36, pp.9–10, at para. 64.
43. UN Document E/CN.4/2000/SR.35 6 July 2000, p.9, at para. 57.
44. Henry F. Carey, 'The Humanitarian Intervention in Haiti and the Development of the Human Rights Regime', *Journal of Haitian Studies*, 1997–1998, Vol.3/4, pp.30–47.
45. MICIVIH Report, 17 June 1994. See Human Rights Watch and National Coalition on Haitian Refugees, 'Rape in Haiti: A Weapon of Terror', New York, 1994.

46. MICIVIH, Press Release CP/94/28, 17 June 1997, pp.34–8.
47. Anne Fuller, 'Challenging Violence: Haitian Women Unite Women's Rights and Human Rights', *Bulletin of the Association of Concerned Africa Scholars*, Spring/Summer 1999, No.55/56 (Special Issue on Women and War), pp.45–7.
48. All elected bodies were suspended by President René Préval on 11 January 1999, who then ruled by decree until autumn 2000.
49. Only three of 80 deputies in the lower house were female; all 27 senators were men; all nine Supreme Court members; and 121 of 127 mayors. Only one of 20 parties are led by a woman. Hans Mardy, *Miami Herald*, 18 July 1999.
50. Terms of Reference, Office of Gender Affairs, UNMIK.
51. UNIFEM helped finance the evaluation.
52. 'Morning Edition', National Public Radio, 30 October 2000.
53. UNSC Resolution 1271 of 25 October 1999 establishing UNTAET does not mention gender mainstreaming. UNTAET's budget is only $15.3 million, compared with $3 billion spent in Haiti and $5 billion in Bosnia.
54. Sherrill Whittington, 'UNTAET: Gender Affairs', 5 November 2000.
55. Ibid.
56. Ibid.
57. Derek Silove, 'Conflict in East Timor: Genocide or Expansionist Occupation?', *Human Rights Review*, Vol.1, No.3, April 2000, pp.62–79.
58. UN Document A/55/305-S/2000/805.7.
59. UN Document A/55/1, pp.8–13.
60. UN Document A/54/405.
61. Celestine Yamou, Presentation, American Society for International Law, Washington, DC, April 2000.
62. UN Document A/55/57/Add.1 at 2, based on UN Document JIU/REP/2000/1 and UN Document A/55/57. The latter says international civil service 'is not subject to any domestic legal system' and that most human rights norms 'are not incorporated into the United Nations internal regulations and rules'.
63. www.unifem.undp.org.
64. UN Document A/54/224 and UN Document, CDAW/SP/2000/2.
65. UN Document CEDAW/C/2000/I/2.
66. UNSC Resolution 1315 of 14 August asked the Secretary-General to negotiate a special international tribunal whose jurisdiction would include crimes of sexual slavery, sexual violence against women and girls, and other war crimes. Angela King, UN Document S/RES/1315 (2000).
67. UN Document S/2000/878/Add.1. Another Secretariat note insists that KFOR personnel follow international law and operational procedures. UN Document A/55/282 at paras 134–5.
68. UN Document E/CN.4/1999/68/Add.1 and UN Document E/CN.4/2000/SR.35, p.12 at paras 77–80.
69. UN Document Supplement No.36,A/55/36, p.4.
70. Hilary Charlesworth, 'The Gender of International Law', in John Lawrence Hargrove (ed.), *On Violence, Money, Power and Culture: Reviewing the Internationalist Legacy*, Washington: American Society for International Law, 2000, p.207.
71. See pessimistic analysis of Elizabeth Riddel-Dixon, 'Mainstreaming Women's Rights: Problems and Prospects Within the Centre for Human Rights', *Global Governance*, Vol.5, No.2, April–June 1999, pp.149–71.
72. Gay J. McDougall writes: 'In all respects and in all circumstances, sexual slavery is slavery and its prohibition is a *jus cogens* norm'. UN Document E/CN.4/Sub.2/2000/21, p.4 at para.9. Kelly D. Askin, 'Sexual Violence in Decisions and Indictments of the Yugoslav and Rwandan Tribunals: Current Status', *American Journal of International Law*, Vol.93, No.1, Jan. 1999, pp.97–123; Barbara Bedont and Katherine Hall-Martinez, 'Ending Impunity for Gender Crimes under the International Criminal Court', *The Brown Journal of World Affairs*,

Vol. VI, issue 1, Winter/Spring 1999, pp.65–85; and Patricia Viseur Sellers and Kaoru Okuizumi, 'Intentional Prosecution of Sexual Assaults', for symposium on 'Prosecuting International Crimes: An Inside View', *Transnational Law and Contemporary Problems*, Vol.7, Spring 1997, pp.45–80.

73. Halima Embarek Wsarzazi noted, 'With regard to female genital mutilation, substantial progress has been achieved since the Sub-Commission in 1983 adopted resolution 1983/1 taking on a problem then considered a taboo. This taboo has been shattered.' UN Document E/CN.4/Sub.2/2000/17, pp.15 at para.79.

Sexual Violence in Times of War: A New Challenge for Peace Operations?

INGER SKJELSBÆK

The image of a raped woman gazing quietly into a television camera from the BBC or CNN has become an icon of the wars in the 1990s. At the time, we, the viewers, knew that while we were staring into this woman's eyes more women were being raped. Despite this knowledge and the press coverage there was little we could do to help. Although these acts of violence were not new in the history of warfare, they appeared to play a new strategic role in the wars of the 1990s, a role the international community was not able to identify nor had adequate response to.

The 1990s was a decade that started with enthusiasm and optimism for the future. The Cold War was over, new democracies were blooming and some of the long-lasting conflicts in Latin America and Africa came to an end. Perhaps we were blinded by these changes so we did not see the contours of a new kind of conflict pattern emerging.[1] Displays of national pride and symbols in, for instance, post-communist countries, were regarded as a positive change. Little did we know in 1990 that it would be precisely these national signs and symbols that would be formative for a new kind of war. In the newly named wars of ethnic conflict the goal was to eradicate or move groups of people belonging to particular ethnic groups from a particular territory. These were wars of identity where friends and family could turn against each other simply by recognizing that the Other was a Serb, Bosniak, Hutu or Tutsi. These were wars where the civilians were the prime target and where the weapons of war were not the latest in military technology, but knives, Kalashnikovs and rape.

In the Brahimi Report of August 2000, which evaluates the current status of UN peacekeeping operations, it is stated that the UN must do its utmost to prevent the failures of the past. In particular the report emphasizes the UN's failure to prevent the genocide in Rwanda in 1994 and to protect the inhabitants of Srebrenica in Bosnia and Herzegovina in 1995, as peace operations that were particularly unsuccessful.[2] One of the challenges the UN did not meet was to protect thousands of civilian women from being raped and otherwise sexually abused by the perpetrators in the conflicts. At the time these crimes were not considered political acts and they were not integral in political analyses of the conflicts. Today we can see that these crimes were indeed part of strategic warfare, and the International Criminal Tribunal for the Former Yugoslavia (ICTY) as well as the International Criminal Tribunal for Rwanda (ICTR) are mandated to investigate these crimes as such.

As the media coverage of the use of sexual violence in the wars in Rwanda and in Bosnia and Herzegovina increased, it became important to ask how this kind of violence was situated compared to other conflicts. Was the situation in these two conflicts unique, or was it simply that these conflicts received the most attention? This was the starting point of the literature survey carried out in 1998 and the beginning of 1999 on which this contribution is based. How was sexual violence described in the 1990s; what conflicts were covered; how was sexual violence used in the respective conflicts and how was the theme described/conceptualized? The study focuses on how sexual violence can be conceptualized and how it was described in articles written in the 1990s, surveying conflict areas in Africa, Latin America, Asia and Europe. Five hypotheses from feminist research on the use of sexual violence in war are then described. The contribution concludes with a discussion of the challenges this form of warfare creates for peace operations.

What is Sexual Violence?

The term 'sexual violence' is most often associated with rape, but the scholarly literature asserts that sexual violence, both in times of war and during peace, is a multifaceted phenomenon, as some examples of sexual violence in wartime may help illustrate. In 1992 Korean women dared for the first time to come forward and testify that between 1932 and 1945 they had been forced into prostitution by Japanese military personnel. Japanese soldiers had forced, lured and kidnapped women into sexual slavery in all the areas occupied by Japanese forces. These women were often very young and came from rural, lower-class backgrounds. Among those who have come forward, many have testified that, after 1945, they could not have children, or that they had chosen not to have any. A life in isolation, in fear of letting others know the truth, has been the reality for many of these women. In Uganda women have been forced to marry men in the rebel forces in order to provide sexual favours for free.[3] Palestinian women in Israeli-occupied territories have told how they have been sexually humiliated by Israeli security guards who fondled them and threatened them with sexual violence.[4] In Somalia, female prisoners have been stripped naked in front of male guards as a means of punishment.[5] In Bosnia, men have been ordered to bite off the testicles of fellow male prisoners, a charge against Ducan Tadic.[6] Sexual violence then is a term which may also include forced prostitution, sexual slavery and genital mutilation.

Second, the term 'sexual violence' suggests that it is an act of violence. 'Rape is not a question of sex, it is first and foremost an act of aggression with a sexual manifestation,' argues Catherine Niarchos.[7] Wars are characterized by the use of various forms and instruments of violence, applied to achieve certain strategic and political goals. Throughout history, sexual violence in times of war has not been perceived as violence on the same level as for instance torture or killings. This perception has excluded the possibility that sexual violence can have a strategic purpose in a conflict situation. The wars in Bosnia and Rwanda have challenged us to think differently.

Third, sexual violence has certain characteristics which distinguish it from other kinds of violence. Sexual violence is always a question of involuntary sexual contact. Rape has been defined as 'physically forceful attempts at sexual intimacy when one of the individuals involved chooses not to become sexually intimate.'[8] This definition captures only the physical aspects of rape: it fails to include the symbolic power aspects embedded in the act. Feminist theory explains a society's risk of rape as a result of the male domination of socio-political and economic affairs.[9] Rape is not perceived exclusively as a violent sexual act: it is also a manifestation of power. This power structure has certain distinguishable characteristics. The perpetrator/victim relationship is normally a male–female relationship, in both war and peace. However, since men can also be victims of sexual violence, the perpetrator–victim relationship ought to be considered as one related to masculinity/femininity rather than strictly male/female. This masculinity/femininity relationship is further embedded in a heterosexual hegemonic power structure where masculinity is what gives power and femininity is void of power. When a man is sexually abused, one could argue that he is feminized and the male perpetrator is masculinized.[10]

How then should we distinguish between the use of sexual violence in times of war and times of peace? It may occur in war for exactly the same reasons as in peace. However, war situations create a further dimension which can become intertwined with the power distinction outlined above. The enemy structure of a given war may make women and men of certain ethnic/religious/cultural groups more 'attackable' than others. Examples include the estimate that between 900,000 and 110,000 German women were raped by Russian forces in Berlin during the final days of the Second World War, and that 20,000 Chinese women were raped in Nanking following the Japanese takeover of the city in 1937.[11] In the former Yugoslavia between 10,000 and 60,000 women, of various ethnic groups, may have been raped.[12] In Rwanda, it is believed that between 250,000 and 500,000 women, predominantly Tutsis, were raped.[13] In a war situation, the logic of the aggressors appears to be that the men and women who have become powerless are seen as 'rapable', and those who have been raped become feminized and ultimately more powerless. This can help explain why most rape victims are women; they represent the most powerless of the powerless.

In addition, it is often women who keep communities and families together, and who are often the primary transmitters of culture. Through their upbringing of children, they ensure that cultural norms and values are transmitted from one generation to the next. When women are the prime targets of sexual violence it must be understood against this background. It seems plausible that the perpetrators want to strike out at the cultural roles of women. This leads to an understanding that the primary target for sexual violence in war is not the individual victim themselves, but the social identity they represent. This acknowledgement creates particular challenges for peacekeeping operations. In order to fully understand the conflict in which a peacekeeping operation is deployed, the role of women, both culturally and politically, must be adequately analysed. Only then can one begin to grasp the workings of wartime sexual violence and thereby define appropriate responses. Ensuring a gender balance among peacekeeping personnel may be one way of approaching this problematic field, simply because it may be easier for victims of this particular kind of violence to approach a female peacekeeper than a male one.

The Use of Sexual Violence in Different Conflicts: Some Examples

Africa

According to Joni Seager, systematic rape was used in the conflicts in Angola, Liberia, Malawi, Mozambique, Somalia, Sudan and Uganda, but few are documented.[14]

Africa Watch has documented the use of rape in a *refugee camp situation* in northeastern Kenya where an estimated 200,000 Somali refugees live. Because men have been killed or have disappeared, there is a high proportion of female-headed households in the camp. In societies where a woman's safety is dependent on having a male protector, refugee camps are far from safe retreats from the conflict zone. For half of the women who reported being raped in the camp, rape was a factor which had caused them to flee in the first place. Most of the rapes reported within the camp were gang rapes, and often repeated rapes, although it was not always the same people committing the rapes. The perpetrators were most often *Shiftas* – Somali Kenyan or Somali bandits who enter the compound and threaten the refugees with looting, beating and killings in addition to rape. But among the rapists were also Kenyan police, security officials and fellow refugees. The rapes seem to have commonly taken place during the night, when herding goats or collecting firewood outside the camp or sometimes – although this is said to be relatively rare – during Kenyan police interrogation. Some of the women have reported that ethnicity – clan identity – was significant as often they were first questioned about their ethnicity before being raped. In other words, if the woman was from the same clan as the rapist/s, she could be spared.[15] The widespread practice of genital mutilation in Somali culture adds to the physical injuries caused by the rapes, resulting in the destroyed possibility of having children.

One of the most horrific uses of sexual violence in war is found in genocide situations. The Human Rights Watch report *Shattered Lives: Sexual Violence during the Rwandan Genocide and its Aftermath* (1996) describes this. According to the UNHCR, as many as 500,000 women are thought to have been raped during the 1994 genocide in Rwanda. The Human Rights Watch report documents rape against both Tutsi and Hutu women, although it emphasizes that the majority of the rapes were directed against Tutsi women in an attempt to destroy Tutsi culture. The report states that, in the build-up to the genocide, political propaganda played on stereotypes of especially Tutsi women, who were said to be more beautiful than Hutu women, and were therefore considered able to infiltrate Hutu ranks by flirting with Hutu men. Tutsi women were also portrayed as being more sexually desirable and daring than their Hutu counterparts. These stereotypes, coupled with the view of woman as man's possession, made Tutsi women particularly vulnerable to sexual violence. Many of the rapes were reported as having been committed by the *Interhamwe*, the Hutu militia, and the military and civilian authorities also took part in these crimes. A pattern of repeated rapes and gang rapes appears to have been the norm.[16] The International Criminal Tribunal for Rwanda (ICTR) delivered the first verdicts in an international court where rape was included as a part of genocide. According to the press statement:

> [T]he Trial Chamber underscored the fact that rape and sexual violence also constitute genocide in the same way as any other act, as long as they were committed with intent to destroy a particular group targeted as such. The court held that sexual violence was an 'integral' part of the process of destruction of the Tutsi ethnic group. 'The rape of Tutsi women was systematic and was perpetrated against all Tutsi women and solely against them', the Chamber concluded. Furthermore, these rapes were accompanied by a proven intent to kill their victims.[17]

The Mayor of Taba commune, Jean Paul Akayesu, was convicted on charges of genocide and crimes against humanity.[18]

The aftermath of the 1994 genocide has been difficult for the women of Rwanda. In 1996 women constituted 70 per cent of the population; half of all households were headed by women, which adds an economical burden to many women. A Human Rights Watch report estimates that between 2,000 and 5,000 children were conceived through rape. These children go by the name of 'children of hate'.[19] Both the raped mother and her child are often socially stigmatized. Furthermore, because HIV and AIDS are an integral part of the impact of rape, since the genocide there has been a tremendous increase in HIV, although exact figures are not specified.

The Americas

Many conflicts in the Americas ended in the early 1990s, making this decade more peaceful than the 1980s. Still, there are areas of major guerrilla activity, such as Guatemala, Colombia and Peru.[20] According to Seager, systematic rape of women and children by soldiers has also taken place in this region of the world.[21] The articles and publications in the literature study cover Argentina, Chile, El Salvador, Guatemala, Peru and Uruguay. This is probably far from all the data available. One practical problem is that much of the analysis and documentation of these crimes in this region has not been translated into English.

Ximena Bunster-Burotto attempts to provide a general overview of how various forms of sexual torture have been experienced by women in the region, by focusing on the situation for women in Argentina, Chile and Uruguay. One common denominator here is that sexual torture was performed by military personnel during interrogation or in detention. The vast majority of victims were women who had become politically active and who were related to men who were politically involved. Sexual torture is intended to instigate fear and humiliation, and Bunster-Burotto offers elaborate analyses of how this particular kind of torture plays upon the traditional gender roles in Latin American culture. According to Bunster-Burotto, the use of sexual violence in patriarchal, macho-dominated societies acts to reinforce the ideological subordination of women in the family and in society at large.[22] In addition to the political goals, she argues, this social aspect was one of the main goals, to humiliate independent and intellectual women who challenged men. Gang rape, repeated rapes and rape in addition to other forms of cruel treatment and torture appear to have been common. Further information can be found in the report of Argentina's National Commission on Disappeared People (1986), which investigated the fate of the thousands of people who disappeared during the military dictatorship from 1976 to 1983. Sexual torture and rape were integral parts of these crimes. Several of the male torture victims reveal how their genitals were mutilated and/or tortured during 'interrogation'. The same was true for the female victims, but they also experienced rape to a seemingly greater extent than their fellow male *desaparecidos* (the disappeared). This report clearly demonstrates that one must take care not to view rape and sexual violence in isolation from other types of torture, because these forms of violence often go together.

Human rights reports on the situation in Peru point to the conceptual difference in regarding sexual violence in war as *torture* or as a *war strategy*. Amnesty International provides detailed accounts of human rights abuses in the areas in Peru where a state of emergency had been declared in 1988. The report clearly defines rape as torture and argues that women of all ages and social classes were very vulnerable to sexual abuse in the emergency zones. The rapes took place after women and children had been separated from their men, when women were being held in detention, or when women simply happened to be in the wrong place at the wrong time.[23] Human Rights Watch, on the other hand, sees rape as a possible weapon of war. Their Peru report investigates how sexual violence was used by both the security forces and the Shining Path. They seem to have detected a pattern where the security forces employed rape as a means of weakening what they considered to be oppositional persons in the conflict. 'Information collected … suggests that rape by the security forces threatens all women equally, but that four elements characterize women who are at greater risk of actual attack: race, social class, occupation, and the explosive mix of gender and armed insurgency particular to the Shining Path and its female cadre.'[24] They conclude that in Peru certain women were targeted for strategic reasons. Of course, the distinction between rape as torture and rape as a strategic weapon of war is more of an academic discussion than a substantial qualitative difference, since for the individual victim the pain and scars are the same regardless of definition. Still, the label we put on such acts has consequences for the perpetrators. Rwandan Mayor Jean Paul Akayesu would not have been convicted if the ICTR had not defined sexual violence as an integral part of genocide. It is noteworthy that two of the leading international human rights organizations have conceptualized the use of sexual violence in the same conflict in such distinctly different ways.

Asia

The majority of the articles and publications from this region focus on conflicts that took place prior to the 1990s. Ten of the 16 items surveyed focus on Japan and the Second World War. Even though these events took place more than half a century ago, it was not until the 1990s that the sexual misuse of women during this conflict became known.

An example of how rape has been employed as a strategic weapon to force inhabitants to flee can be found in reports focusing on the situation in Kashmir, which is inhabited by a predominantly Muslim population. According to Asia Watch, rape by the Indian security forces has been used as a tactical weapon to humiliate and punish the entire community to which the individual woman belongs. Asia Watch strongly urges that the pattern of impunity must be stopped; even though rape is punishable under Indian law, no police officers or members of the security forces have been convicted of rape.[25] Asia Watch suggests that female officers should be encouraged to assist during investigations because this would make it easier to obtain testimonies from rape victims. A further report describes how the first reports of rape emerged soon after the Indian government's crack-down on rising violence by Kashmiri armed militant groups began in 1990. The incidents of rape follow a pattern seen in many other conflicts: soldiers enter the homes of civilians, order the men to leave or to be killed, and then they rape the women. The report provides numerous cases that exemplify this pattern, most of them presented together with the comments/reactions of the Indian authorities who systematically deny that such rapes have taken place. Occasionally the rapes have been investigated, but this report also confirms that no one has been sentenced, so such acts are carried out with impunity.[26]

The *comfort women* issue seems to be the best-documented phenomenon in Asia. The term 'comfort women' is a euphemism for what several authors have called sexual slavery and/or forced prostitution.[27] About 200,000 women were drafted as sex slaves by Japanese soldiers during the Second World War, the great majority (80–90 per cent) Korean, but others were from the territories of Taiwan, Manchuria, Sakhalin, Guangdong, Myanmar, the Philippines, Indonesia, Malaysia, Sumatra and Papua New Guinea.[28] Women from the Japanese islands of Honshu and Hondo, Hokkaido and Okinawa were also 'recruited', as well as Dutch women.[29] Sancho (1997) explains that the system was initiated by Japanese military personnel in order to prevent rape by Japanese soldiers, and also to provide them with free sexual favours and prevent the spreading of venereal diseases. As such the use, and indeed misuse, of these women was considered a 'military necessity'.[30] In the military record, these women were simply listed under the heading of 'military supplies'.[31] As the military records did not list them individually, it is extremely difficult to know how many women were coerced, where they were during the conflict, and where they came from. Neila Sancho also argues that the Japanese military had a hidden political agenda – to crush the spirit of the occupied population, to subjugate and annihilate other Asian peoples whom the Japanese felt were racially inferior.[32] The 'comfort women' were kidnapped from their families, sometimes under promises of a better future, and were then detained in brothels where they experienced the most horrible treatment. Consecutive rape, lack of food, diseases, grave humiliation and physical injury are all described in the testimonies provided to the Executive Committee International Public Hearing concerning the post-war compensation of

Japan, held in Tokyo on 9 December 1992. The half-century of silence was due to factors such as shame, guilt and suicide of the victims and patriarchal and elitist attitudes of the South Korean government, explains Chunghee Sarah Soh.[33] In turn, the Japanese authorities have responded that they have paid for their misdemeanours through the Tokyo Trials, and have no intention of apologizing for anything beyond that. Some of the authors attempt to understand how such a system of sexual slavery could come into being; and how so many people who knew about it never made an outcry. Chin-Sung Chung explains that the heritage of the Japanese imperial system, coupled with a patriarchal social structure, made it easy for Japanese soldiers to draft vast numbers of lower-class Korean women into sexual slavery,[34] and Chizuko Ueno claims that Confucian patriarchy, which urges women not to go public with stories of rape, must take some blame for the 50-year-long silence.[35]

Europe

After the secession of Croatia and Slovenia from Yugoslavia in 1991, and of Bosnia and Herzegovina (BiH) in 1992, Europe witnessed atrocities in the form of ethnic cleansing that many thought had ended with the Nazi Holocaust. The exact number of casualties, refugees and internally displaced persons will never be known. An integral part of ethnic cleansing has been the use of sexual violence. Roy Gutman of *Newsday* reported as early as July 1992 that he had visited a concentration camp in Manjaca in northwestern Bosnia where he witnessed sexual violence used against Muslim prisoners by Serb captors. When he later learned about other concentration camps, among them the notorious death camp Brocko Luka, he discovered that women were held as prisoners, and witnesses told him that these women had been raped. The same was true of the camps in Vogosca, Omarska and Tronopolje.[36]

According to a European Fact-Finding Team, more than 20,000 Muslim girls and women had been raped in BiH since the fighting began in 1992.[37] The report of the Coordinative Group of Women's Organizations of BiH, on the other hand, estimates that the figure could be as high as 50,000; yet other reports estimate that as many as 60,000 women have been raped.[38] The collection and publication of such figures sparked off a chain reaction of hatred and hostility in which Muslims, Croats and Serbs all took part – and which, in turn, led to more rapes being committed.[39] Manipulating the rape figures became a powerful tool in political mobilization.

Rape was committed in concentration camps, in rape camps, in public places and in private homes. The target groups of sexual violence fall into three main categories: (1) girls and women of childbearing age, (2) females either too old or too young to have children, and (3) men. UNICEF's 1996

State of the World's Children report states that teenage girls were a particular target in BiH. Girls were made pregnant and then forced to bear the 'enemy's child', by keeping them imprisoned long enough to ensure that abortion would be impossible.[40]

Rape of females who could not become pregnant fell into two categories: very young girls and elderly women. Girls younger than 15 often died or became permanently disabled as a result of consecutive raping, and young girls and elderly women were often raped in front of family members and friends, and/or publicly in towns and villages.[41] There is relatively little information on how men have been subjected to sexual violence in this war. It is known that men have been raped and otherwise sexually assaulted, but estimates about the exact number seem impossible to make. In the concentration camps, some Muslim men were ordered to rape Muslim women and mutilate each other.[42]

Many writers are concerned about placing these crimes within an international legal framework. The jurisdiction of the International Criminal Tribunal for the Former Yugoslavia (ICTY) is to investigate (1) grave breaches of the Geneva Convention of 1949, (2) violations of the Laws or Customs of War, (3) genocide, and (4) crimes against humanity. There is a strong consensus that the work carried out in the ICTY is an extremely important test case for future tribunals for future conflicts. This work has demonstrated many difficulties, especially concerning controversies involving more general disagreement about the targets of these crimes. Is it a crime of gender – that is, are women targeted first and foremost because they are women – which amounts to a gender or sex crime?[43] Or is it a crime of ethnicity – that the women are targeted because they belong to specific ethnic groups?[44] Another problem is the archaic language of the legal texts themselves. Several authors have pointed out the difficulty in associating crimes of sexual violence with the victim's (the woman's) honour:

> The Geneva Conventions characterize rape as a crime against the honor and dignity of women. ... Women's 'honor' has traditionally been equated with virginity or chastity. Loss of honor implies the loss of station or respect, reinforcing the social view – often internalized by women – that the raped woman is dishonorable.[45]

The argument is that such a conceptualization shifts the focus away from the violent acts themselves to the chastity of the women. And similarly: who 'owns' the woman's honour? Who defines what an 'honourable woman' is?

Why Sexual Violence?

It is not easy to explain why aggressors in a conflict situation resort to the use of sexual violence. With advanced military technology, it seems likely that aggressors would prefer to use weapons which increased the distance between perpetrator and victim. And yet, when we look at the conflict patterns of the 1990s, we have seen a pattern of increased intimacy between aggressors and victims. How can this surprising tendency for aggressors to involve themselves and their own bodies as a part of the aggression be explained? What do they expect to achieve by using this kind of violence?

As yet, little empirical research has been carried out, but some 'facts' can be established. First, the war in Bosnia has shown that sexual violence in war should not be perceived exclusively as an outcome of individual aberration: it is a systematic weapon of war. The mass rapes suggest that the aggressors are not aberrant individuals, but normal people who find themselves in abnormal situations where common norms of behaviour no longer apply. Second, the use of systematic rape in a war situation seems more prevalent in conflicts of identity than in other types of conflict. From this we may conclude that the use of sexual violence aims at targeting the victim's identity – whether gender, ethnicity, religion or other identities. Third, sexual violence appears to be an effective way of removing groups of people from a given territory.

It is important to realize that sexual violence does not happen in a vacuum; it is usually followed by other forms of violence such as torture or killings, making it hard to isolate the consequences. What we can observe is that the use of sexual violence in addition to other kinds of violence accelerates the effects. Ruth Seifert[46] has outlined five theses or interpretations of the use of sexual violence in war, revealing the multifaceted nature of such a study.

First, sexual violence can be seen as an *integral part of warfare*. Seifert argues that, throughout history, there has always been violence against women of the conquered territory, evidenced by the Nanking and Berlin examples cited above.

Second, sexual violence can be seen as an *element of male communication* – the symbolic humiliation of a male opponent. This is based on the understanding that men protect women and that a woman is a man's possession. In a conflict situation, when a man rapes a woman of the 'other side', this act communicates that the husband/father of the woman is unable to protect not only the individual woman, but also his property, his country, his nation.

Third, sexual violence can be seen as a way of *reaffirming masculinity*. Military conduct is dependent on loyalty to the cause and loyalty among soldiers. Militarism is further based on the reduction of individual identity. The military has always felt threatened by idiosyncratic sexual expression (gays/lesbians) deviating from the accepted norm. As Cynthia Enloe explains: 'The glue [of militarism] is camaraderie, the base of that glue is masculinity'[47] – and here one might add heterosexual masculinity. One way of ensuring masculine solidarity among soldiers is to exclude women and homosexuals from the military. In most countries where women have been accepted in the military, this process has been preceded by intense debate. Militaries need 'real' men. Being a real man means, in this context, being able to suppress feelings of insecurity, gentleness and other characteristics which are commonly considered feminine. A combination of these processes makes it easier for men to commit sexual violence in war situations. For example, the majority of testimonies of raped women in BiH reveal that they were subject to gang rape.[48] Group pressure makes it difficult for an individual soldier to refuse rape, because this would reveal 'weakness', or even a deviation from the militaristic heterosexual norm.

Fourth, sexual violence can be seen as a way of *destroying the culture of the opponent*. In the ethnic cleansing process in Bosnia, the goal has been to destroy, or at least deport, members of other ethnic groups. Rape, for instance by Serbs against Muslim and Croatian women, has been a catalyst in this forced migration process. Silva Meznaric points out that rape used as a means of sharpening the edges between ethnic groups in the former Yugoslavia is not a new phenomenon. The rapes in Kosovo from 1986 to 1990, where Albanian men were accused of large-scale raping of Serbian women, led the republic of Serbia to modify its penal code. 'Sexual assault on citizens of different nationalities and ethnicities was considered more aggravating than "regular" rape'. According to Meznaric, this indicates that heterosexual rape had become a political act.[49] The politicization of sexual violence is interconnected with notions of male/female relations. Women are often seen as the biological bearers of a given culture and/or ethnic group.[50] When women's procreative abilities have been manipulated either by forced pregnancy or by making it impossible for girls to have children in the future, the biological basis for a given nation is destroyed. This 'genocidal rape' reduces the identity of the individual woman to her procreative abilities; the cultural identity of the woman is undermined.[51] For the individual woman, however, the situation may be different. For her, not only having to bear the enemy's child (thereby attributing the ethnicity of the rapist to the child), but also nurturing it for years to come, may be life-long torture.

Fifth, sexual violence can be seen as an outcome of *misogyny*. Although the use of sexual violence in the war in BiH has been systematically aimed at non-Serb groups, Serbian women have also been raped. Thus 'women are raped not because they are enemies, but because they are the objects of fundamental hatred that characterizes the cultural unconscious and is actualized in times of crisis'.[52] Studies of refugees support Seifert's claim: the use of sexual violence increases among refugees, in terms of both domestic violence and 'public' violence,[53] because there is an increase in the level of frustration which is taken out on the weak.

Seifert's theses demonstrate that perceptions of sexual violence as a weapon of war should not be regarded as deviations from the heterosexual hegemony in which we all live, but rather as strategic manipulations of that same hegemony.

Challenges for Future Peace Operations

As this overview has shown, the use of wartime sexual violence is far from unique to the conflicts in BiH and Rwanda. It is a form of violence that is used in symphony with other forms of violence in order to achieve particular political purposes. It is an effective weapon of war because it plays on the gender roles of the given society in which it occurs and as such strikes at the core of human interaction; namely male and female relations. It could be argued that future peace operations will not be successful unless ways of dealing with wartime sexual violence are incorporated into the policy planning of these operations. Assistance to traumatized individuals and local communities is increasingly becoming an everyday in-theatre challenge of current multifunctional peace operations. Healing the wounds of sexual violence is extremely difficult. Letting victims be heard, punishing perpetrators and condemning the violence may be steps in the right direction.

There are two developments that indicate that peace operations are moving in the right direction to meet the challenge. First, the emphasis made in the Brahimi Report that more effort should be put on the civilian component of peace operations. In the recommendations by the Panel it is said that '[t]he Panel recommends a doctrinal shift in the use of civilian police, other rule of law elements and human rights experts in complex peace operations to reflect an increased focus and strengthening rule of law institutions and improving respect for human rights in post conflict environments.'[54] The strengthening of these civilian components may make victims of sexual violence less hesitant to report the crimes and get the adequate help they deserve. Second, and this point is linked to the first, the peace operations which have the strongest civilian focus also appear to have the highest percentage of women.[55] The Kosovo crisis showed that, because female human rights experts with Bosnian rape victim experience were in the refugee camps in Albania, they were able to help Albanian rape victims from Kosovo at a much earlier stage than was the case in Bosnia. In the report from the United Nations Food Programme, it is stated that it was not uncommon for victims of rape to prefer talking to a woman representing the international community than to fellow refugees about the violence they had suffered.

Many challenges remain, but it is clear that the historical silence which has long overshadowed this wartime phenomenon has been broken, and that sexual violence is an aspect of warfare that can no longer be ignored by international efforts of conflict resolution.

ACKNOWLEDGEMENTS

I would like to thank PRIO colleague Greg Reichberg for interesting and encouraging discussions and comments on the draft. I would also like to thank the Norwegian Research Council and the programme 'Forced Migration and Resource Conflict' for having funded the first ten months of this project. I am also indebted to the Nansen Fund and the Norwegian Ministry of Foreign Affairs for having funded the remaining three months of the project. A theoretical analysis of the literature referenced here will appear as 'Sexual Violence and War: Mapping Out a Complex Relationship', *European Journal of International Relations*, Vol.7, June 2001.

NOTES

1. See Espen Barth Eide, '"Conflict Entrepreneurship": On the "Art" of Waging Civil War', in Anthony McDermott (ed.), *Humanitarian Force*, Oslo: PRIO Report 4/97, 1997, pp.41–59; and Hjalte Tin, *A Typology of Civil Wars*, Århus: Centre for Cultural Research, Århus University, Denmark, 1997.
2. Report of the Panel on United Nations Peace Operations, A/55/305-S/2000/809.
3. Olivia Bennett, Kitty Warnock and Jo Bexley, *Arms to Fight, Arms to Protect: Women Speak out about Conflict*, London: PANOS, 1995, p.96.
4. Amnesty International, *Women in the Front Line: Human Rights Violations Against Women*, London: Amnesty International Publications, 1991, p.22.
5. Ibid.
6. See James Walsh, 'Was it a Real "War"?', *Time Magazine*, 19 May 1997, p.21.
7. Catherine N. Niarchos, 'Women, War, and Rape: Challenges Facing the International Tribunal for the Former Yugoslavia', *Human Rights Quarterly*, Vol.17, 1995, p.650.
8. Lee Ellis, *Theories of Rape: Inquiries into the Causes of Sexual Aggression*, New York: Hemisphere, 1989, p.1.
9. Ibid., p.11.
10. Silva Meznaric, 'Gender as an Ethno-Marker: Rape, War and Identity in the former Yugoslavia', in Valenatine M. Moghadam (ed.), *Identity, Politics and Women: Cultural Reassertion and Feminism in International Perspective*, Boulder: Westview, 1994, pp.76–97. See also Dubravka Zarkov, 'War Rapes in Bosnia: On Masculinity, Femininity and Power of the Rape Victim Identity', in *Tijdschrift voor Criminologie*, Vol.39, No.2, 1997, pp.140–51.
11. Ruth Seifert, 'War and Rape: A Preliminary Analysis', pp.54–72 in Alexandra Stiglmayer (ed.), *Mass Rape: The War Against Women in Bosnia-Herzegovina*, Lincoln, NE: University of Nebraska Press, 1994, pp.54, 64.
12. Cheryl Bernard, 'Rape as Terror: The Case of Bosnia', *Terrorism and Political Violence*, Vol.6, No.1, 1994, p.29; Adam Jones, 'Gender and Ethnic Conflict in ex-Yugoslavia', *Ethnic and Racial Studies*, Vol.17, No.1, 1994, p.117; Michael J. Jordan, 'Rape as Warfare', *Transition*, Vol.1, No.20, 1995, pp.20–21; 'Rape as a Weapon of War', *Refugees*, August 1993, p.42; Dorothy Q. Thomas and Regan E. Ralph, 'Rape in War: Challenging the Tradition of Impunity', *Sais Review*, Vol.14, No.1, 1994, p.93; Alexandra Stiglmayer, 'The Rapes in Bosnia-Herzegovina', in Stiglmayer (ed.), *Mass Rape: The War against Women in Bosnia-Herzegovina*, London: University of Nebraska Press, 1994, p.85.
13. Human Rights Watch, 'Shattered Lives: Sexual Violence During the Rwandan Genocide and its Aftermath', New York: Human Rights Watch, 1996, p.24.
14. Joni Seager, *The State of Women in the World Atlas*, London: Penguin, 1997, p.56.

15. Africa Watch, 'Seeking Refuge, Finding Terror: The Widespread Rape of Somali Women Refugees in North Eastern Kenya'. Report by Africa Watch Women's Rights Project, *Divisions of Human Rights Watch*, Vol.5, No.13, Oct. 1993.
16. See pp.16, 19, 41–2, 48 of the report (n.13 above).
17. UN ICTY press statement, http://www.un.org/News/Press.
18. Ibid.
19. Human Rights Watch (n.13 above), p.3.
20. Dan Smith, *The State of War and Peace Atlas*, London: Penguin, 1997, p.50.
21. Seager (n.14 above), p.56.
22. Ximena Bunster-Burotto, Bunster-Burotto, 'Surviving Beyond Fear: Women and Torture in Latin America', in June Nash and Helen Safa (eds), *Women and Change in Latin America*, South Hadley, MA: Bergin & Garvey, 1996, pp.302–7.
23. Amnesty International, *Caught Between Two Fires – Peru Briefing*, London: Amnesty International Publications, 1989.
24. Human Rights Watch, 'Untold Terror: Violence Against Women in Peru's Armed Conflict', Report by Americas Watch and the Women's Rights Project, New York: Human Rights Watch, 1992, p.16.
25. Asia Watch, 'Rape in Kashmir: A Crime of War', *Asia Watch & Physicians for Human Rights*, 9 May 1993, pp.1, 5–6.
26. Asia Watch, 'The Human Rights Crisis in Kashmir: A Pattern of Impunity', *Asia Watch & Physicians for Human Rights*, June 1994, p.1.
27. Chin-Sung Chung, 'Wartime State Violence against Women of Weak Nations: Military Sexual Slavery Enforced by Japan during World War II', *Korean and Korean/American Studies Bulletin*, Vol.5, No.2/3, 1994, pp.15–27; Neila Sancho, 'The "Comfort Women" System during World War II: Asian Women as Targets of Mass Rape and Sexual Slavery by Japan', 1997, in Ronit Lentin (ed.), *Gender & Catastrophe*, London: Zed, 1997, pp.144–54; Chunghee Sarah Soh, 'The Korean Comfort Women: Movement for Redress', *Asian Survey*, Vol.36, No.12, 1996, pp.1226–40; George Hicks, *The Comfort Women: Japan's Brutal Regime of Enforced Prostitution in the Second World War*, New York: Norton, 1994.
28. Alice Yun Chai, 'Asian-Pacific Feminist Coalition Politics: The *Chongshindae/Jugunianfu* ('Comfort Women') Movement', *Korean Studies*, No.17, 1993, p.70.
29. The Executive Committee International Public Hearing, 'War Victimization and Osaka-shi, Japan: International Public Hearing Report': Executive Committee International Public Hearing, 1993; Sancho (n.27 above).
30. Christopher L. Blakesley, 'Atrocity and Its Prosecution: The Ad Hoc Tribunals for the Former Yugoslavia', in Timothy L.H. McCormack and Gerry J. Simpson (eds), *The Law of War Crimes*, The Hague: Kluwer Law International, 1997, pp.201–2.
31. Chai (n.28 above).
32. Sancho (n.27 above), p.147.
33. Soh (n.27 above), p.1227.
34. Chung (n.27 above), 1994.
35. Chizuko Ueno, 'The Japanese Responsibility for Military Rape During World War II', *Asian Studies Review*, Vol.17, No.3, 1994, pp.102–6.
36. Laura Silber and Allan Little, *The Death of Yugoslavia*, London: Penguin Books/ BBC, 1995, p.249; Roy Gutman, *A Witness to Genocide*, New York: Macmillan, 1993, p.xi.
37. Figures presented in UNICEF document *The State of the World's Children 1996*. Internet version http://www.unicef.org/sowc96pk7sexviol.htm.
38. Figures presented by Silva Meznaric, 'Gender as an Ethno-Marker: Rape, War and Identity in the Former Yugoslavia', in Valentine M. Moghadam (ed.), *Identity Politics and Women: Cultural Reassertion and Feminisms in International Perspective*, Boulder, CO: Westview, 1994, pp.76–97. Elenor Richter-Lyonette, of the Geneva-based NGO Women's Advocacy, reported 60,000, at the FOKUS seminar in Oslo, 17 June 1996. Neither Meznaric nor Richter-Lyonette comments on the ethnic composition of these figures.
39. The information in this paragraph is based on Vesna Nikolic-Ristanovic's paper 'From Sisterhood to Non-Recognition: Instrumentalization of Women's Suffering in the War in the Former Yugoslavia', presented at the conference *Women's Discourses, War Discourses*, at the

Ljubljana Graduate School of the Humanities, 2–6 Dec. 1997.

40. http://www.unicef.org/sowc96pk7sexviol.htm.
41. Beverly Allen, *Rape Warfare: The Hidden Genocide in Bosnia–Herzegovina and Croatia*. Minneapolis, MI: University of Minnesota Press, 1996, p.101; Jill Benderly, 'Rape, Feminism, and Nationalism in the War in Yugoslav Successor States', in Lois A. West (ed.), *Feminist Nationalism*, London: Routledge, 1997, p.65; Bennett *et al.* (n.3 above), p.8; Meznaric (n.38 above), p.92; Stiglmayer (n.12 above), p.82.
42. See Silber and Little (n.36 above), p.245.
43. See, e.g., Jennifer Green, Rhonda Copelon, Patrick Cotter and Beth Stephens, 'Affecting the Rules for the Prosecution of Rape and Other Gender-Based Violence Before the International Criminal Tribunal for the Former Yugoslavia: A Feminist Proposal and Critique', *Hastings Women's Law Journal*, Vol.5, No.2, 1994, pp.171–82.
44. C.P.M. Cleiren and M.E.M. Tijssen, 'Rape and Other Forms of Sexual Assault in the Armed Conflict in the Former Yugoslavia: Legal, Procedural, and Evidentiary Issues', *Criminal Law Forum*, Vol.5, No.2–3, 1994, pp.471–506.
45. Rhonda Copelon, 'Gendered War Crimes: Reconceptualizing Rape in Time of War', in Julie Peters and Andrea Wolper (eds), *Women's Rights, Human Rights*, New York: Routledge, 1995, p.201.
46. Seifert (n.11 above), pp.57–66. Susan Brownmiller, *Against Our Will: Men Women and Rape*, Harmondsworth: Penguin, 1975, p.35, supports this analysis.
47. Cynthia Enloe, *The Morning After*, Berkeley, CA: University of California Press, 1993, p.52.
48. Bennett *et al.* (n.3 above), pp.231–51; Stiglmayer (n.12 above), pp.86–147.
49. Meznaric (n.38 above), p.86.
50. Spyros A. Sofos, 'Inter-ethnic Violence and Gendered Constructions of Ethnicity in Former Yugoslavia', *Social Identities,* Vol.2, No.1, 1996, p.64.
51. Allen (n.41 above), p.100.
52. Seifert (n.11 above), p.65.
53. Bridget Byrne, 'Towards a Gendered Understanding of Conflict', *IDS Bulletin*, Vol.27, No.3, 1996, pp.31–40; Lillian Comas-Díaz and Mary A. Jansen, 'Global Conflict and Violence Against Women', *Peace and Conflict: Journal of Peace Psychology*, Vol.1, No.4, 1995, pp.315–31.
54. Summary of Recommendations, 2(b). Peacebuilding strategy, http://www.un.org/peace/reports/ peace_operations.
55. See Anita Helland and Anita Kristensen, 'Women in Peace Operations', in Helland *et al.* (eds), *Women and Armed Conflicts*, Oslo: Norwegian Institute for Foreign Affairs, 1999, pp.80–81.

Military Women in Peace Operations: Experiences of the Norwegian Battalion in UNIFIL 1978–98

KARI H. KARAMÉ

Background

In 1978 Israel invaded Southern Lebanon up to the Litani River in order to stop Palestinian infiltration and attacks into its northern regions. After the withdrawal of the Israeli forces the UN Security Council agreed upon sending peacekeeping forces to Lebanon. The first contingents of the United Nations Interim Forces in Lebanon (UNIFIL) arrived in the area in March 1978. UNIFIL consisted of military forces from several countries, around 5,000 persons in all, who were deployed from the Mediterranean coast in the west to the Syrian border in the east. Besides multinational tasks, each country was given the responsibility for one particular region.

The mandate given to UNIFIL was to restore the authority of the Lebanese State, to supervise the withdrawal of the Israeli forces and to re-establish international peace and order. In 1984 a fourth point was added to the mandate: to provide security and humanitarian assistance to the civil population.

UNIFIL was born as a result of Security Council Resolution 425, adopted against the will of Israel. The Lebanese authorities, on their side, worked hard for the establishment of a peacekeeping force, but was not one of the fighting parties, which involved Israel, the Palestinian Liberation Organization (PLO) and three to four smaller Palestinian factions. Some Lebanese joined the Palestinian side, while a mainly Christian militia, led by Major Haddad of the Lebanese Army, had contacts both with Israeli and Lebanese authorities. The Shi'a Muslim party Amal also had their armed wing in the area, and after 1982 the more combatant Shi'a militia of Hizbollah (God's Party), backed by Iran, were more and more present as well. Israel backed the South Lebanese Army (SLA) which in the beginning consisted mainly of Christian soldiers from Major Haddad's division, but which recruited a growing number of Shi'a Muslims. When Israel withdrew from South Lebanon in May 2000 approximately 70 per cent of the SLA soldiers came from the Shi'a community. The peacekeeping forces therefore had to face an extremely complicated situation, both formally and on the ground.

Problems with fulfilling parts of the mandate soon became obvious, as Israel did not withdraw completely and also started to establish a local militia. As a reaction to both these factors, Lebanese resistance movements arose, often in collaboration with Palestinian forces. Israel therefore invaded Lebanon for a second time in June 1982 and this time up to Beirut, while Palestinian camps both in the north and in the Bekaa valley were heavily shelled. The Palestinian political leadership had to leave the country, taking with them the major part of their military forces and equipment. Israel withdrew its forces once more, but this time the forces remained in a so-called security zone along the border, with an enlargement in the eastern area where the Israeli, Syrian and Lebanese borders meet.

The Israeli-occupied zone thus became a region of complicated co-existence between some of the UNIFIL forces, Israeli forces, their local proxies, a growing resistance movement and the Lebanese civilian population. The region put under the responsibility of the Norwegian battalion (NORBATT) was entirely included in the occupied zone.[1]

The United Nations and Women in Peace Operations

Since the early days of the United Nations the concept of gender mainstreaming, generally understood as introducing awareness of the status of women into the public arena,[2] has been on the agenda of the organization, but usually as a marginal question. After the UN declared Decade for Women, 1975–85, demands were heard for making gender a factor in the development assistance performed by the organization. Finally, after the Beijing conference in 1995, requests were made for mainstreaming gender in all of the UN activities. For most researchers the concept of gender today includes both male and female roles. But as peacekeeping is still a male-dominated area, the focus here will be on women.[3]

All peace operations under the auspices of the United Nations have included a number of women, mainly in the medical corps. As peace operations have been looked upon and constructed as military operations, the number of posts women could hold were limited, since very few countries admitted women in military functions up to the 1980s. Norway is still one of the few countries where women's participation in the military is completely open and where women can serve in all functions. A multinational peace force will therefore consist of nations having different traditions and policy concerning women in armed forces. As the position of force commander is supposed to rotate among the contributing countries, the women in military posts may suddenly experience exclusion, at least as long as the United Nations does not work out clear guidelines for what posts they may hold. The final report from the Secretary-General concerning the implementation of

Resolution 425 of 19 March 1978 did not mention women's eventual participation in the peacekeeping operation in South Lebanon, and therefore, logically enough, nothing about the posts they might hold.

Contact with the Host Society

Over the 20 years of NORBATT, from March 1978 to December 1998, more than 30,000 Norwegians served in South Lebanon. The large majority were men but there were also a certain number of women, representing from 3.3 to 6 per cent of the troops. The area they deployed in had been partly deserted by its population, which had decreased from more than 20,000 to 5,000 persons.[4] The area was heavily devastated by the war, lacked vital services like health care and infrastructure, regular water supply, electricity and telephone. If ever repaired, the infrastructure was often subject to sabotage.

Just after their arrival the soldiers lived in tents, but they later moved into houses whose owners for various reasons had left the area. This resulted in very close and constant contact with the local population on several levels, and from day one of deployment. The presence of the UN soldiers reassured the population, it resulted in the return of many of the inhabitants who had sought refuge elsewhere, and also created jobs. UNIFIL became the biggest employer in the South and engaged more than 350 persons on a regular basis as secretaries, translators and so on, of whom 13.6 per cent were women.[5] In addition a parallel economy grew up, based on the services to the UN soldiers. Whereas the jobs offered by UNIFIL existed all over the area, but mainly around the headquarters in Naqoura, the extent of the service business depended on the personal economic means of each nation's soldiers. Compared to other nationalities the Norwegians were well paid, and in addition to that they came from a very expensive country, making shopping in Lebanon very attractive for them. Business soon flourished, combined with bars, cafes, restaurants and even a small hotel. The presence of the peacekeepers created a sense of confidence, even if they could not assure total security. The inhabitants appreciated them as witnesses to and reporters of an eventual outbreak of violence. Land and roads were cleared of mines, if not totally, at least to an extent that made it possible to grow vegetables and fruit, and keep some sheep and goats. Both the material and economic situation improved, and gradually part of the population started to return.

An expression of the close relations that grew up between the peacekeepers and the local population is the many marriages that were contracted between young Lebanese girls and foreign soldiers, mainly from European countries. In the small town of Ebl-es-Saqi alone, which housed one of the biggest Norwegian camps, some 25 young girls married Norwegian soldiers.[6] There is no research or organized information about these marriages, but several former

NORBATT soldiers and the priests who always accompanied the troops, indicate that the number could be around 100 in all, including both Muslim and Christian brides. This attraction between two extremes, North and South, on the one side men coming from a country known for its liberal social conventions and on the other girls with a very traditional family-orientated background, is at least surprising. It may almost be seen as a miracle that no serious related incidents have been reported. It is possible that there was some kind of pressure or 'push factor' from the Lebanese parents – in Lebanon emigration has been looked upon as a solution both to economic and political problems since the second half of the nineteenth century, and has been escalating since 1975. Marrying a foreigner, something which is usually not easily accepted by Lebanese parents, may therefore have been seen as a positive way out of a very difficult, not to say hopeless, situation. Many brothers and sisters have followed the young woman to her new country, and some of the couples plan to settle in South Lebanon when they grow old, or at least spend part of the year there. No marriages are known between Norwegian female peacekeepers and Lebanese men. This can probably be explained by the demographic situation in the area, which again resulted from the fact that men had to leave the NORBATT area to avoid being recruited by the SLA. It was also very difficult for the Norwegian women to engage in informal contact with a Lebanese that might lead to a love affair. They ran the risk not only of being misunderstood by the Lebanese men, but also of being criticized by their fellow Norwegians, both men and women.

The well-equipped NORBATT contingent provided free medical and dental care. Many of the soldiers used their time off from service to help the local population repair their damaged houses and gardens, churches, mosques and schools. This help was very much appreciated because it was understood as a token of the soldiers' concern for the ordinary men, women and children. On the other hand, the contingent used humanitarian assistance in a conscious way to establish a positive co-existence with the host society.[7] UNIFIL was conceived and organized as mainly a military peacekeeping operation, but because of the many relationships that grew up between the local population and the soldiers, it took on more and more of the aspect of the third generation of peace operations, the multifunctional. These are supposed, in addition to establishing security, to assist in the rebuilding of the civil society and in the reconstruction of the infrastructure.

In return, the peacekeepers could perform their patrols and control functions without having to look over their shoulders all the time. The close contact with the host society was also an important source of direct or indirect information on what was going on. Some people would see it as their duty to tell the peacekeepers about movements on the terrain, whereas the soldiers, on the other hand, could more easily sense tension in their surroundings. One of the duties of the peacekeepers was, for instance, to see that no arms or ammunition were brought into their area. But those locals who were affiliated to one of the militias were sometimes very imaginative in avoiding checkpoint controls. It has been told, both by locals and by former NORBATT soldiers, that fake funerals were even arranged where the coffin was used to transport illegal items.[8] And as will be shown below, local women were wily about avoiding being searched, as the soldiers at the checkpoints were mostly men.

Women in NORBATT

The nature of functions that women were allowed to occupy changed radically over the years. In Norway there is compulsory military service for men, whereas since 1977 women have been allowed to serve on a voluntary basis and to apply to military schools and colleges. Since 1984 women have had equal rights with men in the Norwegian armed forces, which means that they can hold combat posts and command in the field. From 1978 to 1984 the women in NORBATT therefore served in the medical corps, logistic and staff units, but from 1984 onwards a steadily growing number applied for military posts. There was considerable discussion concerning women's presence in military functions, both in Norway, within NORBATT and within UNIFIL on a more general level, and feelings ran high.

The main concerns and aims of any peace mission are of course the fulfilment of the mandate and the security of the personnel, whether men or women. The most frequent reasons given against women in military functions have always centred around their security; it was felt that their comrades could not bear to see them wounded or killed and that this would in return affect the morale of the entire troop. Luckily, the Norwegians never had that experience. Furthermore, it was supposed that women would not be able to act with authority, for instance at checkpoints and on patrol rounds, in contact with men from a different cultural and religious background. The female peacekeeping soldiers, on the other hand, seem to agree that people saw and reacted to the uniform, and not to the sex. Sometimes they also had the feeling that their presence at a checkpoint lowered the tension.[9]

When they were off duty, women soldiers would often go and see the local women, sit and talk about women's issues and sip coffee.[10] They talked about the problems they faced in everyday life, about worries and hopes. These visits led to friendship between Lebanese women and Norwegian women peacekeepers, which in turn became part of a general mutual confidence building. They further generated a better knowledge of what was going on in the host society, which as we have seen was important for UNIFIL, both for the fulfilment of the mandate and for the security of the troops.

The women in the Norwegian battalion shared a problem with most women who work in male-dominated professions. Working together was not a problem, but it was more difficult to share interests when off duty. The women often feel a kind of loneliness because they represent a minority within a majority with whom they do not share the same interests or ideas of what to do with their free time. This was particularly acute because NORBATT was deployed over their area of responsibility in military camps on a manning scale from some hundreds to four soldiers. The women compensated for this by arranging meetings once a month for 'women only', where both officers and private soldiers came together and where they discussed questions of particular interest for them, for instance how to have women appointed as field commanders.[11]

Description of the Host Society

The NORBATT area was complicated not only because of the security situation resulting from occupation and the presence of several militias. Its population is estimated to be about 20,000 persons belonging to different religious communities, Shi'a Muslims estimated at around 60 per cent of the total population, some Sunni Muslims, Druzes around 20 per cent, and the rest Christians: Greek Catholics, Maronites and some Greek Orthodox. The number of Christians in the area has been going down since before the outbreak of the war in Lebanon, and is today estimated at around 20 per cent. The inhabitants live in small towns or villages, usually with a religiously mixed population, dominated either by Christians or Muslims. Many of them are peasants, but all through the occupation a small number of Lebanese civil servants continued to live there.

A Female-dominated Population

Unemployment, security reasons, but mainly the risk of being forced to join the SLA militia, made many young men leave the occupied area at the age of 14–16, to stay in other parts of the country or to emigrate. Women, children and old people therefore constituted the majority of the population. More than 25 per cent of the households were headed by women, compared to 14 per cent on a national level. Many of the women were the main breadwinners of the family as their husbands and sons did not always find work outside the area.[12] The jobs offered by UNIFIL and the service business towards the soldiers represented welcomed income sources for many of these women, first and foremost because of the money, but also because it was socially accepted to work for UNIFIL or with the soldiers. One of the rare alternatives was to go to work in Israel, but those who did might get into trouble with the militias who were hostile to Israel. After the liberation of South Lebanon some women were convicted for cooperating with the enemy, even if this consisted only in working for instance on Israeli farms.

Lebanese Women's Participation in the War

One of the most frequent arguments used against the presence of women in military functions in peace operations is that it might offend local culture or religion. In this context it is therefore useful, not to say necessary, to look at what Lebanese women actually did during the war. Lebanese society is described as both traditional and patriarchal, by most authors using a gender perspective or interested in women's condition.[13] Even if most of the women during the war were busy keeping their family together, or took on new roles in civil society, all political movements and also their military wings – the militias – included a certain number of women.[14] Most of them served in support functions, but some also served in military posts. Their presence in political rallies and parades, whether in uniform or not, was of high symbolic value. It was a message sent out to the world that they were all in this together.

Unlike the male combatants, women often took on several roles. The story of Mrs Jaradi may serve as an illustration. When her husband, a leader of the Amal organization, was murdered by the Israelis in 1984, she involved herself in the resistance. She worked as a nurse and also smuggled ammunition under her clothes. She recounts how at night women would sit in groups on hills or on the top of the buildings to keep watch; they would warn the men whenever the enemy approached. Sometimes women and girls made barricades out of burning tyres in order to block off the streets so that the men could escape. Support roles – according to Mrs Jaradi – include the smuggling of food and weapons (pregnancy was a popular disguise), keeping watch, and creating a diversion so that men could get away, and finally explaining to the families and neighbours what was going on. And if they had to carry arms, they would do it. Otherwise their role was primarily social and educational.[15]

Stories about women's performance in combat proliferated as the war went on. A building in downtown Beirut was called the 'Girls' building' because it was held by a group of young female combatants of the mainly Christian Lebanese Forces for several months during the first 'round' of the war, which lasted from April 1975 to the end of 1976.[16] Around 3,000 young girls and women received military training by the Lebanese Forces, and 250 to 300 young women fought in their ranks for several years.

The Lebanese were therefore used to seeing women in uniform, both on the streets and in rallies and parades, and photographed in newspapers and magazines, on television and in films. The stories of their activities were told and retold during the long vigils of the war, in shelters and wherever people gathered. It was a hot subject because people's opinion on whether it was in accordance with good behaviour for a girl to be a combatant ranged from disgust to admiration.[17] In any case, it was a generally known phenomenon, and it would not come as a surprise to UNIFIL's host society to see – and even to communicate with – women peacekeepers in military functions. This author therefore finds that local culture, traditions or religion should not so easily be used to exclude women from military functions in peace operations. Better knowledge is recommended, or, preferably, use of already existing knowledge and experience.

Whether women should hold military functions in peace operations or not may also be posed as a question of security, both for the peace forces and for the situation in the area of responsibility. As seen above, local women do not hesitate to smuggle ammunition and to carry arms, if necessary. But women were also involved in more dubious actions, like placing explosives and booby-trapped cars in the Israeli-occupied area. Such acts were usually called 'suicide actions' as the perpetrators were sometimes blown up with the car. They were considered martyrs of a Holy War by the members of the Shi'a resistance, and many believed that they went directly to Heaven. One Umm Hamad, who had already lost three sons in the war, tells about her youngest daughter who 'went on a mission against the Israelis in 1988'. She was captured and held in a prison in the south of Lebanon. After two years they stopped having news about her. She was just 17 years old. Before she was captured, her mother had overheard her asking the Sheikh during a lesson in Islam: 'Is a suicide mission a sin?' Because of this question, Umm Hamad supposed that her daughter had been involved in a so-called suicide action.[18] There are several similar stories; one of them has even been filmed, but they are not easy to verify. Our conclusion must be that women should also be searched for security reasons, and only other women can do that.

New Force Commander, New Gender Policy

In 1992 the Swedish General-Major Lars Erik Wahlgren was appointed force commander of UNIFIL. He had a negative attitude towards women serving in a number of functions, like guard and patrol duties. The functions they could still be assigned to were the staff unit, medical and technical services. The recommendations he sent out to the participating countries represented an enormous change in opportunities for the women in UNIFIL, particularly for the Norwegian women who by then had also been serving in the military for several years.

The overwhelming maleness of national military forces is replicated at the international level. Peacekeeping is not explicitly referred to in the UN Charter, and each mission will, in a way, be specially designed. The former Secretary-General Boutros Boutros-Ghali recommended to the General Assembly in 1995 a target of 50 per cent women in UN field missions, but achievement of this goal is dependent upon the inclusion of women by member states contributing troops.[19] Boutros-Ghali most probably meant women both in civilian and military functions, but it is still interesting to find that over the years the share of women in military posts serving in UN missions has increased only to little more than four per cent.[20]

The new force commander explained his attitude by his concern for negative reactions that might come from Muslim and Druze men. But he had no evidence to point to. What shocked the Norwegian women soldiers and officers even more was the attitude of the Norwegian office selecting the personnel for service in UNIFIL, who did not question this change in policy. The spokesman for this office declared that the UN had full right of disposal over the Norwegian forces, and that they had to follow the UN decision. They did not ask whether this policy was in accordance with the basic guidelines of the whole UN system. The spokesman of the Army's headquarters expressed a more nuanced point of view, regretted that there was no time to bring this question up on a national political level and hoped for guidelines both from the UN system and from the politicians before recruiting for the next contingent.

The leader of the Committee of Defence in the Norwegian Parliament sided with the force commander, telling the women and the nation to either adapt or withdraw – quite a responsibility to put on the shoulders of young women who just wanted to do a job they knew they were qualified for, that many already had experience of and, above all, felt that they had the right to. The Ministry of Defence declared that they would not exercise cultural imperialism, and provoke the local population by using women in military functions.[21]

Norwegian women officers did not submit to this attitude, but started a campaign in the media at the same time as they lobbied the political parties. The network for women officers and the inspectors for women's affairs in the Norwegian armed forces were particularly active, together with women officers with experience from UNIFIL and other UN operations. The whole situation was a clash between contradictory attitudes, where only the women officers seemed to use their experience from the field, whereas many of their male colleagues seemed hesitant to confront the new force commander.

At the same time, the (woman) Norwegian Major Britt T.B. Brestrup served as head of department on a UN mission in the peace zone between Iraq and Kuwait, after having served in Lebanon. Later, she became the first woman observer on the Golan Heights. In Kuwait, she headed a multinational unit composed of 20 persons, seven of them women. She told Norway's biggest newspaper that she did not find it problematic to be a woman on duty in a Muslim country: 'When I arrive in uniform they conduct themselves in accordance to that.'[22] Other women sided with her on this, and explained that as long as they behaved according to normal Norwegian standards, Muslim and Druze men would show them respect. Some even argued that Norwegian men who are used to treating all women as their equals, and are brought up together with girls, face much bigger problems in relation to local girls and women and their male relatives.

In a paper published in 1997 Brestrup quotes a conversation she had with a (male) officer from Pakistan, who was her superior in Iraq. When he asked her why she had never applied for service in Kashmir, she explained the Norwegian army's attitude against sending women to Muslim countries. He was very upset and told her bluntly that he was tired of Western countries using religion to cover up for their own attitudes.[23]

In their struggle for the right to serve in UNIFIL, the Norwegian military women could also have pointed to the fact that many countries with a Muslim majority, or who define themselves as Muslim states or republics, have women in their armed forces, and some of them even serve in combat positions. 'Iran, Iraq, Syria, Indonesia and Nigeria are some of the nations in which Muslim women serve in single-sex or mixed-sex military units. Some are assigned to combat positions (Iran) or internal security posts (Pakistan), while other militaries assign women support roles (Indonesia and Palestine)'.[24] Best documented is probably the case of the women in the armed forces in Libya, where a Military Academy for women was opened in 1979. In his Green Book, written in the years 1977–79, General Qaddafy presents his ideas about the Jamahirya (the State of the Masses) where he sees a role for both men and women in the defence of the country. He states: 'It is the right and a duty for every Libyan man and woman to carry weapons.' Women were supposed to defend themselves, while the men defended the long borders of this enormous country.[25]

The end of this story was that the Norwegian women officers succeeded in their struggle to continue to serve in international peace operations on equal terms with their male colleagues. In an advertising campaign in 1994, the Norwegian armed forces' office for recruitment invited both men and women to enlist for service in UNIFIL. The opposite would have been a serious blow to the possibility of Norwegian women having a career in the armed forces, because participation in international operations is seen as a condition for advancement. When equal rights for women and men were adopted by the armed forces in Norway in 1984, the target was to have an average of 15 per cent of women among the military personnel by the year 2000. This has not been achieved by a long way, since only a little more than three per cent of the professional officers are women, and 5.5 per cent when all the enlisted are included.

Conclusion

During their 20-year-long presence in South Lebanon, the Norwegian battalion always included a certain number of women. They served in support functions, and after 1984 also in military posts. Women of both categories played an important role in this mission, which took place under very complicated circumstances: PLO activities until 1982, the Israeli occupation, various Lebanese militias, and the absence of Lebanese authorities.

In addition to losses of human lives and health, the civil population had to face damage of buildings and infrastructure, and the danger of landmines in the fields and on the roads. Young and adult men left the area because of unemployment, and mainly to avoid being forced to join one of the militias. They only paid rare visits to the area. This led to a female-dominated population.

Many Lebanese women took an active part in the long-lasting conflict. Most of them undertook support functions within one of the various militias, they smuggled arms and ammunition, and some also fought with arms. A few also placed explosives or booby-trapped cars inside the Israeli-occupied zone. One of the reasons women and even young girls were used in this kind of operation is said to be that they were usually not searched at checkpoints, where mostly men were posted.

Any peacekeeping force has two main concerns: the fulfilment of their mandate and the security of the troops. A good relationship with the host society is of basic importance in both these aspects. Since the majority of the local population are often women, and since women as we have seen may be actors on different levels in the conflict, it is essential to have women personnel among the peacekeepers, both in civil and in military functions.

During the last few years the UN system has become more demanding and outspoken concerning equal rights for women in all fields. The need for more women in peace operations is no longer a subject for discussion. Current and future peace operations will have more civil and fewer military components, and will therefore most probably include more women than in UNIFIL. This will only happen, though, when a target of having a greater share of female personnel is included in all stages of the process, from the planning, through the formulation of the mandate, and to the recruitment to a peace mission. Military personnel will always be the first to enter an area of conflict, where the security situation may still be very unstable. They will most probably meet a population with a majority of women, even more than in South Lebanon. The presence of women among the military personnel will consequently be of great importance during this phase, to establish positive contact with the host population, and thereby contribute to the preparation of the conditions necessary for assuring the security of the troops and the fulfilment of the mandate. Clear guidelines from the UN system concerning which posts women may hold will encourage more women to enlist, and also facilitate their introduction into international peace forces. The matter is too important to be left to individual preferences or decision-making on the national level.

NOTES

1. This part is mainly based on two publications from the UN Veterans' National Federation, Norway, in 1998: *UNIFIL 1978/NORBATT I* and *Fredsbevaring gjennom 50 år* (Peacekeeping throughout 50 years).
2. Cynthia Enloe, *The Morning After: Sexual Politics at the End of the Cold War*, Berkeley: University of California Press, 1993, p.20.
3. Louise Olsson, *Gendering UN Peacekeeping: Mainstreaming a Gender Perspective in Multidimensional Peacekeeping Operations*, Uppsala: Department of Peace and Conflict Research, Report No.53, 1999, p.3.
4. UNDP report on the population in South Lebanon, Beirut: UNDP, 1998.
5. Judith Stiehm, 'Peacekeeping: A New Role for Women Seeking Peace', in Ingeborg Breines, Dorota Gierycz and Betty Reardon, *Towards a Women's Agenda for a Culture of Peace*, Paris: UNESCO, 1999, p.131.
6. Information given by the *mukhtar* (elected mayor) of the town in 1997.
7. Steinar Nygaard, 'Situasjonen for sivilbefolkningen da NORBATT rykket inn i april 1978', in *Fredsbevaring gjennom 50 år*, Oslo: UN Veterans' National Federation, 1978, pp.89–91.
8. Interview 1997, as mentioned above.
9. Lieutenant Bente Sleppen, interviewed by *Aftenposten* (Norwegian daily newspaper), 13 March 1992, among others.
10. Information given by Captain Ingrid Gjerde, Oslo 1999.
11. *Bergens Tidende* (Norwegian daily newspaper), 9 November 1993.
12. UNDP report on the population in South Lebanon, Beirut: UNDP, 1998.
13. Kirsten Schulze, 'Communal Violence, Civil War and Foreign Occupation. Women in Lebanon', in Rick Wilford and Robert Miller (eds), *Women, Ethnicity and Nationalism: The Politics of Transition*, London: Routledge, 1998, pp.150–69. See also Lamia Shehadeh, *Women and War in Lebanon*, Gainsville, FL: University of Florida Press, 1999.
14. Kari H. Karamé, 'Girls' Participation in Combat: A Case Study from Lebanon', in Elizabeth Warnock Fernea, *Children in the Muslim Middle East,* Austin, TX: University of Texas Press, 1995, pp.378–92. Kari H. Karamé, 'Maman Aïda, A Lebanese Godmother of the Combatants' in *Women and War in Lebanon*, pp.195–209. Jocelyne Khweiri, 'From Gunpowder to Incense', in *Women and War in Lebanon,* pp.209–28. Lamia Shehadeh, 'Women in the Lebanese Militias', in *Women and War in Lebanon*. Maria Holt, 'Lebanese Shi'i Women and Islamism: A Response to War', in *Women and War in Lebanon*, pp.145–67.
15. Holt (n.14 above), pp.181–3.
16. Karamé and Khweiri (n.14 above).
17. Karamé (n.14 above).
18. Olivia Bennett, Jo Bexley and Kitty Warnock, *Arms to Fight, Arms to Protect: Women Speak Out about Conflict*, London: Panos, 1995, p.262.
19. Hilary Charlesworth and Christine Chinkin, *The Boundaries of International Law: A Feminist Analysis*, Manchester: Manchester University Press, 2000, pp.293–7.
20. Ibid.
21. The presentation of this debate is based on interviews and reports in various Norwegian newspapers in 1992.
22. *Aftenposten*, 3 August 1992.
23. Britt T.B. Brestrup, 'Kvinner – en viktig ressurs for mangfoldet i multinasjonale operasjoner', in Kari H. Karamé og Torunn L. Tryggestad, *Kvinner, krise og krig*, Oslo: NUPI, No.225, pp.75–83.
24. Kathryn M. Coughlin, 'Women, War and the Veil: Muslim Women in Resistance and Combat', in Gerard J. DeGroot and Corinna Peniston-Bird, *A Soldier and a Woman: Sexual Integration in the Military*, Essex: Pearson Education Limited, 2000, pp.223–40.
25. Maria Graeff-Wassink, *La Femme en Armes: Kadhafi féministe?*, Paris: Armand Colin, 1990, and 'The Militarization of Women and "Feminism" in Libya', in Elisabetta Addis, Valeria E. Russo and Lorenza Sebesta (eds), *Women Soldiers: Images and Realities*, London: Macmillan Press Ltd, 1994, pp.137–49.

Gender Mainstreaming in Practice: The United Nations Transitional Assistance Group in Namibia

LOUISE OLSSON

Among the UN peacekeeping missions over the years, the mission to Namibia in April 1989 to March 1990, called UNTAG (United Nations Transitional Assistance Group), is regarded as one of the most successful. However, ten years before a UN gender policy for peacekeeping was developed, UNTAG demonstrated major advances regarding the incorporation of gender issues. Unlike earlier missions, UNTAG included a substantial civilian component[1] which was mandated to rebuild or create institutions, such as a non-apartheid democracy and a judicial system, including respect for human rights. As the UN mission plan was not gender adapted, many of the women in the civilian UNTAG staff took it upon themselves to adapt their work to meet the local needs of both women and men. This was especially important regarding political rights and human rights, where the low social status of women would limit their access to equal treatment and opportunities. This contribution attempts to show that a gender perspective, in effect, was being mainstreamed. Furthermore, the gender balance became an important issue at the highest level of decision-making in UNTAG. Increasing the number of women was also the target of an informal equality group working within the UN system, the Women's Group for Equal Rights. Some of the work of this group assisted the UNTAG management level in recruiting competent women. As a result, the UNTAG mission showed that it is possible to recruit a large number of competent female UN staff and that women were able to work in all posts in the civilian component of a peacekeeping mission.[2]

This contribution will begin with a description of the UN work for equality at the time when UNTAG was planned and implemented and of the policies which are still under development. It then highlights gender problems that were vital for the UNTAG mission to address, in order to ensure not only the needs of men but women as well. The essay concludes with an assessment of the female participation in the civilian component of UNTAG and an analysis of what could have been learned from the mission regarding gender issues.

UNTAG in the Context of the UN Decade for Women

The road to the final deployment of a UN mission in Namibia was long. The authorization was given in 1978 with UN Security Council Resolution 435.[3] However, it took until 1989 before the operation could be launched. This time period is very interesting from a gender perspective. Running in parallel with the struggle to reach an agreement for Namibia and the development of an UNTAG implementation plan,[4] was the UN Decade for Women (1976–85). The Decade was proclaimed by the General Assembly to ensure that the status of women was elevated in the areas of equality, development and peace. A series of women's conferences were held and at the Third World Conference on Women, in Nairobi 1985, the Nairobi Forward-Looking Strategies (NFLS) were signed. This document was the sum of objectives in the three areas of importance, which had been developed mainly between 1976 and 1985. A delegation of Namibian women participated in the Nairobi women's conference and the NFLS brought up Namibian independence and expressed support for Security Resolution 435. Furthermore, it underlined the need to support local women's movements to enable women to participate fully in a post-independent society. The question of gender-specific aspects of the Namibian conflict was further discussed in the UN's Economic and Social Council (ECOSOC) which even acknowledged that apartheid affected women and men differently. Unfortunately these developments do not seem to have influenced the planning of the operation. It could have created a basis for adapting the UNTAG operation to meet the needs of both local men and women, a policy today termed gender mainstreaming.

Gender Mainstreaming[5]

Gender mainstreaming is the main UN procedure to address gender inequality. A UN definition of gender mainstreaming states:

> Mainstreaming a gender perspective is the process assessing the implications for women and men of any planned action, including legislation, policies or programmes, in all areas and at all levels. It is a strategy for making women's as well as men's concerns and experiences an integral dimension of the design, implementation, monitoring and evaluation of policies and programmes in all political, economic and societal spheres so that women and men benefit equally and inequality is not perpetuated. The ultimate goal is to achieve gender equality.[6]

UN policy states that the gender mainstreaming process requires an assessment policy that does not assume gender neutrality. It is considered important to define all issues in all fields of UN work in a manner which enables diagnosis of the possible consequences for men and women. Moreover, even if gender mainstreaming is to be handled by all parts of the UN organization, gender units and focal points are considered vital to ensure progress and provide expertise. One final principle of gender mainstreaming stresses the importance of a political commitment and the allocation of sufficient human and financial resources. To ensure successful implementation, the main responsibility is placed on the highest decision-making levels. Further, the importance of female participation on these decision-making levels is stressed. The need to increase female participation, that is, to achieve a more even gender balance is thus a complementary objective of gender mainstreaming policies.

Gender Balance

Achieving gender balance in an organization concerns the degree to which men and women work at all levels and in all functions. Article 8 in the 'Charter of the United Nations' states that '[t]he United Nations shall place no restrictions on the eligibility of men and women to participate in any capacity and under conditions of equality in its principal and subsidiary organs'. The present goal of the UN goes a step further and attempts to reach a gender balance of 50 per cent women and 50 per cent men in all professional posts. This has been achieved with a rather high success rate in certain departments. However, balancing gender in field missions appears to be more difficult. Struggling with recruitment problems and the influx of non-UN external personnel, the percentage of women in the civilian component of ongoing multidimensional peacekeeping operations remains below target.[7]

Mainstreaming Gender in Namibia: A Field Level Practice

Strategies for gender mainstreaming call for a greater number of local women to be involved in peace processes. Yet, even though Namibian women had begun to achieve a larger role in Namibian society during the armed conflict, hardly any women were involved in the peace negotiations at the international level. Nor was the UN mandate gender mainstreamed. Instead, it was the efforts of female UNTAG staff which contributed to the development of gender mainstreaming practices in the operation.

Organizing 'Free and Fair' Elections

An issue in the Namibian conflict resolution process, with clear implications for gender equality, was the conduct of free and fair elections organized by UNTAG. Feminist researchers emphasize that men and women live under different conditions and have different opportunities. This made it particularly important for the UN to reach the entire population with information on democracy and election procedures. However, if a peace agreement does not specifically point out the importance of ensuring equality, implementation of special efforts to enable local women to vote can be interpreted as beyond the scope of the mandate. The interpretation of who constitutes 'the people of Namibia' and what constitutes necessary means to enable elections to be free and fair are, therefore, vital in determining suitable actions. Secret ballots might have an effect in and of themselves[8] but, as UNTAG District Director Isel Rivero points out, it is essential to target women with information on exercising their rights. Otherwise only the male half of the population might receive the information on how to exercise their right to vote and consequently, the elections might not be free and fair.[9]

Rivero describes how, at the initial information meetings in Namibia, men would be the only ones participating in debates while women would sit quietly at the back. In order to reach women, then, she used the local societal framework. She organized meetings through the women's wing of the cattle union to which many white women belonged and meetings through the Lutheran Church to which many black women belonged. In this way she could specifically target women with her education on democratic principles, human rights, and women's equal political rights and freedoms. This method of work was then expanded to other districts where female UN staff worked. The effort was supported by the Special Representative of the Secretary-General (SRSG) Martti Ahtisaari, if somewhat unofficially due to difficulties with interpreting the mandate, and facilitated by the SRSG's wife, Eva Ahtisaari, who was in Namibia with her husband.[10] Furthermore, because female UN employees, such as Rivero, had contact with the Namibian women's movement, information which otherwise might not have been collected could reach the SRSG.[11] For example, it had come to Rivero's knowledge that the Herero women in her area were not sure that the vote was secret or that they could vote differently from their husbands. This had created uncertainty among women who feared retaliation at several levels. Through joint briefings with the local churches and with the assistance of a very solid information campaign from UNTAG, announcing that 'the vote is secret', which the SRSG directed, this problem was addressed.[12]

Another problem with awareness training of women was the time factor. Alma Mieze, a Namibian who worked in a Windhoek UNTAG election unit, claims that there was not enough time for the UN to reach all local women. Since there was a very limited knowledge of the meaning of democracy in 1989, and because the illiteracy rate among women was very high, it was impossible to reach all women and convince them of the importance of voting. Due to the limited knowledge of democracy in many countries where the UN is to build peace, Mieze stresses the importance of long-term education and training in combination with the UN work of raising the awareness of local women. Even if this process cannot be completed during the mission, it is still of major significance that it is introduced.[13] A lucid example of information that the UN can provide to the entire population is to include material on the Declaration of Human Rights in the vernacular languages.[14]

Raymonde Martineau, UNTAG Deputy District Director, claims that it is necessary to involve the local population in the planning of the mission and ensure that the local women are included. She sees women as a group being equally affected by the mission but with the least influence over planning and implementation. An operation must interact and learn from the people at a community level as well as bring knowledge to the host population.[15] The Namibian independence period was also the time when women's organizations were developing into independent organizations. The UN, as prescribed by the NFLS, could have considered this development. Lack of interaction with local groups and organizations was also typical of the initial phase of UNTAG, but with time the operational structure was adapted to interact more with local NGOs and political parties.[16]

Creating a New Constitution: Gender Equality before the Law

Traditionally, women had not been 'central' in the domain of public politics in Namibia. Only a few women had ever been appointed to a decision-making position. This was mainly due to the perception that women's place was in the private, rather than the public, sphere. With the struggle for independence, Namibian women came to play a significant role, for example as combatants and trainers in the South West Africa People's Organization's (SWAPO) camps on the Angolan border. This form of female participation has often been seen as constituting a step towards reaching a more gender equal post-independent society. Nevertheless, Heike Becker indicates that a post-liberation society often displays about the same degree of gender inequality as the pre-liberation society. It has been pointed out that since the constitution and the laws remain more or less the same, regardless of the group in control of power, the fundamental situation for women does not change.[17] As Security Council Resolution 435 called for an independent Namibia, the drafting of a constitution was required. This was assisted by international staff to ensure that it was written in accordance with international requirements. This presented an opportunity to make both laws and the constitution gender sensitive.

Upon approval of the Namibian Constitution, the Constitutional Assembly had only one female representative, Pendukeni Ithana, of SWAPO. She was at the same time secretary for SWAPO's Women's Council. To increase the level of gender awareness, Rivero, in cooperation with another important female SWAPO representative, Libertine Amathilda, and the Lutheran Church, organized a sit-in outside the Constituting Assembly to persuade them to include the issue of gender equality as a main paragraph in the Constitution. Out of this collaboration came the recommendation to create an Office for Women's Affairs within the newly created government.[18] In general, many statements concerning the formulation of the constitution have been positive and it seems as if women in SWAPO's organization had an influence on the process. There are, however, certain formulations that women's organizations have been criticizing, for example, the lack of a definition of 'family' in the constitution.[19]

Mobilizing voters and formulating a constitution are only two dimensions with obvious gendered implications not considered by the UNTAG operation but where actions of a more formal nature are needed. The actions taken by female UN employees are, nevertheless, important indicators of how gender mainstreaming might be orchestrated.

A Gender Balanced Civilian Mission Is Born

If the UNTAG operation displays important examples of where gender mainstreaming efforts need to be directed, the mission is even more a precursor regarding gender balance in the civilian staff. Unlike later multidimensional missions of the same generation, the UNTAG mission has been noted for the large number of women in the UN civilian staff, both in field and in decision-making positions. SRSG Martti Ahtisaari and the UNTAG Director-General Cedric Thornberry made conscious attempts to increase the number of women in the mission and deliberately recruited women for decision-making positions. Thornberry points out that peacekeeping missions have almost always included women but because they have been concentrated in the service sector, their presence has not been recognized.

The majority of the UNTAG civilian staff had been recruited from within the United Nations system, and the gender composition in general was much more balanced in the civilian component than in the military component or the police units.[20] Of the civilian staff, about 50 per cent were women.[21] In UNTAG's middle management, the percentage of women in decision-making positions was substantial. Three of the ten regional directors and five of the district directors were women. The number of women in registration and electoral offices was about 50 per cent. Women also served as senior liaison officers to political parties, political advisers to the police as well as troubleshooters working from Windhoek, travelling to the places where they were needed. This type of staff consisted of about 40 per cent women.[22] Moreover, women were not chosen for lighter duty stations even though this had been suggested by certain members at the United Nations Headquarters (UNHQ). Linda Cohen, for example, was appointed regional director of the northern region, which was greatly affected by the war.[23]

The high level of female participation in the Namibian mission was a combination of non-discriminatory recruitment and of the struggle by the UN's informal Women's Group on Equal Rights within the UN system for women to be allowed to go on a peacekeeping mission. When the opportunity arose, due to the non-discriminatory policies of the UNTAG leadership, many of the leading women within the UN system were encouraged to apply for the mission. Many UNTAG women had, therefore, worked on issues of equality before being sent on the UNTAG mission. Both Rivero and Martineau believe that the presence of female UN staff, being considerable in number, affected the success of the mission. In Rivero's and Martineau's experience, UN women tended to be less concerned with hierarchy and more inclined to respect the local population and work together with them to achieve a resolution of the conflict.[24]

Mary Eliza Kimball, Deputy Regional Director of UNTAG in Windhoek, correspondingly supports the view that the precedence of both women and men of different nationalities working together on an equal basis helped set a positive example for increased understanding in Namibia.[25] This was further enhanced, as both Ahtisaari and Thornberry describe, by a strong feeling of mission which developed in UNTAG. This feeling made the staff pull in the same direction, rendering a person's gender or nationality irrelevant. There is often fear at UNHQ that the local population will not accept female UN staff. However, in the case of Namibia, there was little support for this fear. Female UN staff seem to have been accepted by the Namibian population in the same manner as male UN staff.[26] Martineau describes how the local population at first tended to project their own gender assumptions on her, believing her to be the secretary of her male colleague rather than his equal. But this changed as Martineau and her male colleague worked together and the population could see that she too had authority and was treated as an equal. Therefore, Martineau emphasizes the importance of male UN staff treating female colleagues as equals. If they do not, then women's authority becomes undermined with the local population and difficulties arise for female staff performing their duties.[27]

To ensure gender mainstreaming and gender balance of a mission the main responsibility is placed on the leadership. In the case of UNTAG the need for gender awareness at the highest levels is visible as both Ahtisaari and Thornberry considered equal opportunity as vital.

The UNTAG Leadership and Gender Equality

Ahtisaari was selected as SRSG in 1978, and the long period between being selected and the actual mission, especially in combination with Ahtisaari being appointed Under-Secretary-General for Administration and Management in 1987, gave him special advantages concerning the recruitment of personnel that no other SRSG had ever had.[28] In his work as Assistant Secretary of State for Development Co-operation in Finland, Ahtisaari had had many women in his organization and felt that it would have been strange not to involve both women and men in the UNTAG operation. Throughout the operation, women were given tasks according to their experience and capabilities, disregarding prejudiced assumptions about their gender. The situation during UNTAG was not perfect, and there was occasional abuse of power, but the situation was in many ways better in the field. This was dependent on the fact that women were given a chance to 'function as professional, just like men' due to the leadership's decision to not discriminate against women.[29]

The large number of women in UNTAG was, as Ahtisaari points out, not a goal in itself but rather an effect of recruiting with an unbiased method the most qualified and best-suited people within the UN system. But since the attitude at UNHQ at that time did not favour the high percentage of women admitted to serve in UNTAG, the degree of female participation became an issue in itself.[30] The largely unbiased manner in which the personnel were recruited to UNTAG was initially the responsibility of Cedric Thornberry, who was to handle the practical administration both at the UNHQ level before the mission and as Director-General during the mission. Thornberry agrees with Ahtisaari that the design was not outlined to specifically increase the number of women in order to create a gender balance; they had simply asked for volunteers and the best of these were chosen regardless of gender or nationality. When it became well known that the selection process was unbiased, there were volunteers from several of the groups which previously had not been selected for peacekeeping missions, among those women.[31] The recruitment of the best personnel, in combination with the volunteering by many of the women working on gender issues, created a foundation for gender mainstreaming.

Ahtisaari points to several different aspects that impede the increase in the number of women in peacekeeping. One concerns a general problem of finding further employment when the mission is over. Often employees can find themselves without assignments when returning to UNHQ after an operation.[32] Another issue concerns the obstacles for women to advance to middle posts in decision-making in the UN. This complication creates difficulties in raising the number of women in decision-making positions in the field since these often are recruited from within the UN system and placed in field positions related to their positions at headquarters.[33] Thornberry correspondingly states that women seem particularly reluctant to volunteer for field missions. Field experience does not particularly benefit careers at headquarters and can actually have quite the opposite effect as it is necessary to be present at headquarters in order to advance more easily.[34] Moreover, the family situation often places limitations on women, since women do still have the main responsibility for child care, and the opportunity for bringing children on a mission is rare. The UNTAG operation did, however, present a few such cases where children of female staff were granted permission by the leadership to accompany their parent. The positioning of these staff members was then dependent on where child care could be provided. Kimball reported how bringing her children with her on the mission presented her with many connections with the local community which she otherwise might not have been able to establish. These local links then facilitated her work as Deputy Regional Director.[35]

According to Ahtisaari, the attitude of the leadership concerning equality, equal opportunity and non-acceptance of sexual harassment affects the operation as a whole. The staff must feel the leadership has taken a strong stand concerning these issues, and only then can it be ensured that women are given a chance to perform their duties as international civil servants successfully. Ahtisaari describes how he had people of strong integrity and competence, whom he knew personally, in strategic places in the organization. These people were then eyes and ears of the SRSG and his office, and could ensure that the basic guidelines of the operation were being followed. However, considering that other missions cannot be planned as UNTAG was, Ahtisaari emphasizes the importance of selecting a leadership that believes in the basic principles of the operation and will ensure that rules which emphasize the responsibilities of the leadership, such as not discriminating against women, are enforced. Ahtisaari stresses that if the number of women is low enough for the leadership of a mission to be suspected of having a discriminatory attitude toward female personnel, the leadership should answer to the DPKO, where 'feeble excuses' should not be accepted. Furthermore, Ahtisaari points out that it is correspondingly important for the SRSG to feel the support of the Secretary-General in the work for equal opportunities in the mission.[36]

The need for strict guidelines regulating the behaviour of all UN staff, male and female alike, regardless of whether they are civilian, police or military, is pointed out by both Rivero and Martineau. In Rivero's words: 'The UN has to enforce standards that are equal to the mandate it has on equality' and not bring shame to the UN blue beret.' Rivero suggests that the behaviour is best handled with the leadership taking an active part in the enforcement of rules. She gives the example of the Kenyan battalion that was based in her district of Okahandja. At night, accompanied by some of the civilian police, Rivero would go to the district bars to observe how the soldiers on leave were behaving. If their behaviour was not in accordance with UN standards, she would contact the local military commander, who would then remove his troops from the bar. That Rivero and the local Kenyan commander agreed on the need for military troops to behave was a prerequisite for the control of the troops.[37] Likewise, Martineau points out the need for the leadership to take an active part in curbing any unwanted behaviour from the staff. She states that the setting of a good example by the leadership, in combination with strict enforcement of rules and guidelines are necessary if good behaviour by the staff, be they military or civilian, is to be achieved.[38] Thornberry further supports this. He has become more and more convinced of the need for strong leadership in his continued work in peacekeeping missions around the world. He stresses that this concerns both the top and middle management in an operation.[39]

In spite of the attitude of the leadership, a few cases of sexual harassment, or discrimination, did appear during the mission.[40] As an example of the latter, a dilemma arose involving one male UNTAG decision-maker who refused to have a woman working in his office. This man was regarded as important for the mission but his behaviour was not considered acceptable by the leadership. The result was, however, that the woman was moved to another office.[41] UN employee Patricia C. Baigrei, who worked in a district near Swakopmund, gives another example of how the main problem for female UN staff in some cases might have been to work with their male colleagues rather than with the local population. She states that a female colleague of hers was given the post as head of a district. Her deputy was male and refused to accept her decisions or to perform any duties that he considered 'female chores'.[42] The cases of sexual harassment of female UN staff were serious, as Martineau points out, but they did take place in the UN framework where action could have been taken. No particular rules were issued that restricted the behaviour of UN staff on mission but the fundamental rules for staff of the UN, based on the UN Charter, could have been implemented.[43] This is not the case regarding incidences of harassment of local women. Furthermore, the misconduct of UN personnel appeared in an environment where the local women had little or no protection. In addition, many of the local women were in economically vulnerable situations.[44] The attitude and the behaviour of the male staff toward the local women might also affect the treatment of female UN staff by the local population as it sets a discriminatory example.[45]

Toward a Gender Mainstreamed and Gender Balanced Future?

The operations in Kosovo and East Timor are now being conducted under the form of mandate that Namibia had in 1989–90. Both missions include a gender unit which, unfortunately, has been meeting several obstacles to accurate functioning. For example, there has been lack of financial support. In consequence, even if the UN's policies for gender mainstreaming of peacekeeping operations are being developed, they are far from operational. The UN seminar 'Mainstreaming a Gender Perspective in Multidimensional Peace Support Operations' held in Windhoek in May 2000 agreed on 'The Windhoek Declaration and the Namibia Plan of Action'[46] in which several objectives for gender mainstreaming and gender balancing of missions are presented. Some of these objectives were, however, developed in practice about ten years ago to which hardly any recognition has been given.

Despite the discussions in the UN regarding women and peace as early as in the 1970s and 1980s no official effort was made to adapt the UNTAG operation to address the needs of both women and men. As the mission developed, the field staff, predominantly female, began to adapt their work to meet the local needs of both women and men as it became obvious that the implementation plan had flaws regarding gender sensitivity. The gender division in society that made it necessary to target women specifically can perhaps further serve to underline the fact that women-specific programmes and gender units are needed in order to ensure that the UN goal of equality is adequately and sufficiently met. However, as gender awareness developed in the UNTAG hierarchy, the operation as a whole began working with women's organizations. The work to obtain free and fair elections not only regarding race but also regarding gender and the work with a gender-equal constitution displays two important areas in multidimensionality that can be more easily analysed and assessed after the UNTAG operation. This helps the work of defining all UN areas of activity in order to diagnose gender differences.

'The Windhoek Declaration and Namibia Plan of Action' supports the need to analyse the specific effects and to mandate the implementation of gender mainstreaming into post-conflict reconstruction situations. This would be a prerequisite for being successful in increasing gender awareness of the local women as requested by Mieze. To ensure their importance, gender issues should be included in presentations of mission reports to the Security Council and other relevant bodies. The Declaration underlines the need for a gender-sensitive leadership, but as SRSGs today are rarely involved in developing a mission to the same extent that Ahtisaari and Thornberry were, there is more of an emphasis on giving SRSGs in-depth briefings on gender mainstreaming and increasing the number of women SRSGs. The top leadership of UNTAG had great hope that future missions would take after the UNTAG operation on many issues, such as regarding gender balance.

In the case of the Namibian operation, it is possible to begin by observing effects on the mission when a large percentage of female staff is introduced. The UNTAG mission is considered a success in many aspects, especially regarding keeping the peace. It is possible that there exists a correlation between gender composition and mission success. This, of course, has not been examined systematically, but the theoretical implications could be well worth investigating.

UNTAG is a clear case of efforts being made to increase and broaden women's participation in decision-making and in peacekeeping operations. It is especially interesting that this originally was not a deliberate purpose of the leadership. Their goal was to be able to appoint the personnel they considered most competent regardless of gender. Moreover, the UNTAG experience indicates that there seems to be a need for women's organizations within the UN system to help mobilize competent female staff and further underlines the importance of recruitment of gender aware personnel. Many of these aspects are now central to 'The Windhoek Declaration and the Namibia Plan of Action'. It is unfortunate that there was such a substantial time gap between the experiences of the UNTAG mission and the gender mainstreaming policy for peacekeeping being developed. However, applying the lessons learned ten years ago to ongoing and future missions can still be of major significance.

ACKNOWLEDGEMENTS

This contribution is based on the report the author wrote for the UN seminar, Mainstreaming a Gender Perspective in Multidimensional Peace Support Operation, held in Windhoek, Namibia, 27–30 May 2000. The report is published by the Lessons Learned Unit at the Department of Peacekeeping Operations at the UN. The author wishes to thank everyone who contributed, especially Isel Rivero and Martti Ahtisaari, for their valuable help. She also wishes to thank Peter Wallensteen, Mary-Jane Fox, Josabeth Kärre and Torunn L. Tryggestad for their help with this essay. The contents of the essay and the report are, however, the sole responsibility of the author.

NOTES

1. The UNTAG Civilian Police (CIVPOL) was considered a civilian component of the operation at large. However, the focus of this contribution is on those parts of the UNTAG operation that first and foremost were involved in the planning and conduct of the elections.
2. The difficulties in finding competent women and the difficulties for women working in certain field positions are often used as explanations of the low number of women in peacekeeping.

For a discussion on the number of women participating in recent peacekeeping operations see Stiehm's contribution in this collection and also Louise Olsson, 'Mainstreaming Gender in Multidimentional Peacekeeping: A Field Perspective', *International Peacekeeping*, Vol.7, No.3, 2000, pp.1–16.

3. S/Res/435 (1978) approves of the implementation plan for settling the conflict suggested by the Secretary-General's report (S/12869). The plan included the removal of the South African administration and troops from Namibia and the establishment of UNTAG to assist the Special Representative of the Secretary-General in ensuring the independence of Namibia through free and fair elections. The power was to be transferred to the people of Namibia.
4. The main work on developing an implementation plan was concluded around 1978. No women were involved in the planning or in the assessment missions until about three months before the operation was launched.
5. For further discussion, see Judith Hicks Stiehm's contribution in this collection.
6. Chapter IV, Coordination Segment, DESA, New York.
7. For a discussion on the recruitment of women to UN field staff positions see Judith Hicks Stiehm's contribution in this collection.
8. The secrecy of the vote, as observed by UNTAC (United Nations Transitional Authority in Cambodia) volunteer Joakim Öjendal, apparently led to a realization by the Cambodian politicians that women were going to make independent decisions. Families were not allowed to vote together and, consequently, it was up to individual women and men to choose the political party they thought would serve their interests best. Even if the most common scenario in the election campaign was that of a male politician addressing a male voter, the concept of individuality facilitated the participation of women as the need to mobilize female voters arose. Another practical issue that might have contributed to women's registration to vote was that the operationalization of the mandate prescribed that the number of seats in Parliament was to be based on the number of registrations in a certain region. If women were not encouraged to register in one region which was the stronghold of one party, this would give an advantage to parties dominating other regions if they encouraged 'their' women to vote. It is possible that this may have increased the incentive for the political parties to facilitate women's registration considering women's demographically superior number in the age group eligible to vote. In consequence, these indirect factors might have contributed more to women's participation in the elections than any action taken by the UN to facilitate the participation of Cambodians in the elections if not in the political campaign. No similar analysis has been made of the Namibian elections.
9. Interview with Isel Rivero by Louise Olsson in Madrid on 13 April 2000. The interpretation of the mandate was a major issue of conflict. South Africa did on several occasions accuse the UN of overstepping its authority.
10. Interview with Isel Rivero (n.9 above).
11. Interview with Martii Ahtisaari by Peter Wallensteen and Louise Olsson in Helsinki on 3 March 2000.
12. Interview with Isel Rivero (n.9 above). The matter was solved in an unexpected way. Eva Ahtisaari was later that same week asked to give a speech to the women's union of Namibia and being very pressed for time she asked Isel Rivero to take her place at the meeting. Her speech was later reprinted in several newspapers of Namibia and things began to change, a change supported by the SRSG. Without the SRSG's understanding, the matter would have run the risk of being considered to be outside of the mandate and Rivero could have been asked to leave her post.
13. Interview with Alma Mieze by Louise Olsson in Windhoek on 8 June 2000.
14. Isel Rivero found that the people in her area did not have any knowledge of this declaration and therefore, in cooperation with Yale and a South African University, she translated the Declaration into several of the vernacular languages. There was no money for printing these documents and, cooperating with friends, she took it on herself to find ways of distributing this material in her area. Interview with Isel Rivero (n.9 above).
15. Interview with Raymonde Martineau by Louise Olsson in Geneva on 14 April 2000.
16. Conversation with Cedric Thornberry by Peter Wallensteen on 22 April 2000.

17. Heike Becker, *Namibian Women's Movement 1980 to 1992*, Frankfurt/M.: IKO-Verl. für Interkulturelle Kommunikation, 1995, pp.18–23.
18. Interview with Isel Rivero (n.9 above).
19. See Heike Becker (n.17 above), pp.237–41.
20. The overall strength of UNTAG was approximately 8,000 personnel, of which 4,500 were military personnel, 1,500 were police and 2,000 were civilians.
21. Judith Hicks Stiehm, 'Peacekeeping and Peace Research: Men's and Women's Work', *Women & Politics*, Vol.18, No.1, 1997, p.41. The number of women in the Civilian Police and the military components was very low. New Zealand and Canada were two of the few countries which sent female personnel. The UN did not start asking contributing countries for increased numbers of female Blue Berets until 1994.
22. Martti Ahtisaari, 'Statement, Under-Secretary-General for Administration and Management: Women on Mission', 1990. Unpublished manuscript.
23. Interview with Cedric Thornberry by Peter Wallensteen, 4 April 2000.
24. Interview with Raymonde Martineau (n.15 above) and interview with Isel Rivero (n.9 above).
25. Conversation with Mary Eliza Kimball by Louise Olsson on 22 June 2000.
26. This is supported by the interview with Cedric Thornberry (n.23 above), the interview with Ahtisaari (n.11 above) and by the conversation with Mary Eliza Kimball (n.25).
27. Interview with Raymonde Martineau (n.15 above).
28. Interview with Martti Ahtisaari (n.11 above).
29. Conversation with female UNTAG employee.
30. Interview with Martti Ahtisaari (n.11 above).
31. Conversation with Thornberry (n.16 above).
32. Interview with Martti Ahtisaari (n.11 above).
33. Interview with Raymonde Martineau (n.15 above).
34. Interview with Thornberry (n.23 above).
35. Conversation with Mary Eliza Kimball (n.25 above).
36. Interview with Martti Ahtisaari (n.11 above).
37. Ibid.
38. Interview with Raymonde Martineau (n.15 above).
39. Interview with Thornberry (n.23 above).
40. To what degree is classified UN information.
41. Interview with Thornberry (n.23 above).
42. Interview with Patricia C. Baigrei by Louise Olsson in Geneva on 12 April 2000.
43. Interview with Isel Rivero (n.9 above) and interview with Thornberry (n.23 above).
44. Interview with Raymonde Martineau (n. 15 above) and interview with Isel Rivero (n.9 above).
45. Interview with Patricia Baigrei (n.42 above).
46. The document can be found in Appendix I this collection.

Closing Remarks

CYNTHIA ENLOE

A funny thing has happened on the way to international political consciousness: 'gender' has become a safe idea.

We are now in the midst of the second wave of international feminism. The first wave began in the 1840s, as women from France, Germany, the United States and Canada began to trade ideas and strategies in order to overcome the formidable forces opposing women's right to vote. It grew and expanded – though not without debates, misunderstandings and fractures among its activists – as its members from not only North America and Western Europe, but now too from Egypt, Vietnam, Palestine, Latin America and Korea – sought to take on the thorny issues of women's relationships to militarism, colonialism and trafficking in women. By the 1930s, while remnants of this first wave still persisted, it was in tatters as a genuinely international coherent movement. This first wave of international feminism spoke in terms of 'women', 'patriarchy', 'citizenship' and even 'slavery'.

It is the second wave of international feminism that has adopted (though not always by consensus) the concept of 'gender'. Part of the success of the emergent second wave of international feminism has been to put women's lives and feminist questions onto the formal agendas of the foreign policy establishments of dozens of state regimes and international agencies. Thus in 2001, one can utter the word 'gender' – as in 'gender and development' or 'gender and democratization' or 'gender and foreign debt' – in the corridors of the World Bank, the UN Secretariat or the European Commission without hearing someone guffaw (well, at least not out loud).

Still, along with this seeming rhetorical acceptance has often come an unspoken dilution of the potential that this concept of gender has for disputing the institutional mindset. Too frequently these days, 'gender' is used as if it were just a bureaucratically comfortable synonym for women. It is not. Alternatively, 'gender' is used as if it referred only to the crafting of, and enforcement of standards of acceptable femininity (and femininities). This second inclination is a bit better. At least it implies that to introduce questions about 'gender' into any policy conversation is to introduce questions about power. But this second usage of 'gender' still leaves the politics of masculinity (and masculinities) safely off the policy table.

The contributions brought together here, so provocatively cultivated and edited by Louise Olsson and Torunn L. Tryggestad, should provide a valuable antidote to the worrisome presumption that 'gender' is intellectually bland. To take seriously the full implications of gender entails shining bright lights into the cultures, the structures, and the silences of peacekeeping. Reading the contributions that comprise this collection should make us uncomfortable. 'Peacekeeping' should not look the same when we're done. Things that we take for granted now should become disturbingly problematic as we finish reading these seven contributions. The measures we have relied upon to determine the success or failure of any given peacekeeping operation – under UN, OAS or NATO aegis – should have multiplied and been rearranged in their saliency. The skills we have come to believe are the most relevant ones for managing any peacekeeping operation should, by the end of our careful reading here, be redefined.

For instance, if we pursue serious questions – about how exactly in each peacekeeping mission competing notions of 'manliness' shape the interactions between the Canadian military and the Fijian military commanders, between the Swedish military commander and the UNHCR civilian female field staff, between the Ghanaian male army rank and file and the remnants of local paramilitaries, between American male soldiers and international traffickers in prostitution – we should begin to feel destabilized in our own understandings of how and why that peacekeeping operation worked the way it did. We should also probably think about which actors in the conflict zone and which officials and soldiers in the particular international agency and regime have the greatest stake in our not investigating the politics of manliness. Who has the greatest stake in treating presumptions about masculinity as if they were irrelevant, trivial? The answers to 'who has a stake in preserving the silence?' might prove surprising.

The great strength of the preceding essays is that they recognize the need for all of us who are interested in peacekeeping to develop several different levels of analytical curiosity. As the contributions demonstrate, we need to be able to understand and weigh myths; we also have to be able to follow the breadcrumbs of any organization's unwritten internal culture; simultaneously we need to dig deeply into any given present, while we think historically and comparatively. These demands on us for an adequate understanding of how women and men are positioned differently in the fuelling and resolving of societal violence can scarcely be met by any of us working alone. This makes this collective format especially valuable. It allows us to pool our skills, pool our curiosities.

This collection is being published at a particular moment in the ongoing evolution of peacekeeping. First, we all are reading these seven studies at a moment when feminist-informed scholars and activists are putting the causes of militarization high on their own analytical agenda: we know that unless we can figure out just who has a stake, for example, in defining 'respectable femininity' as incompatible not just with combat, but with leading a political party, we are not likely to fashion successful strategies for genuine demilitarization. Second, we are reading and digesting these analyses at a time when many of the governments' military forces that are being called upon to lend troops to peacekeeping operations are themselves being pressed – by the European Court, by local gay rights movements, by coalitions of liberal feminists and liberal legislators – to rethink the conventional notion that masculinity is the *sine qua non* of a modern military. Third, we are all reading the essays at a time when certain armed forces which have prided themselves on effective peacekeeping – and in that pride, have thought of themselves as emblematic of the whole nation's worthiness – have been compelled to confront embarrassing 'lapses' in soldiers' behaviour. One need only think of the current public scrutiny under which have come the Dutch military's 1995 behaviour in Bosnia, the Canadian paratroopers' actions in Somalia, some Italian peacekeeping soldiers' behaviour in Mozambique, and certain German troops' actions in Bosnia, to realize that peacekeeping can be the source of both governmental and national soul searching.

We are always writing and reading in history. There is a chance that if we each read the whole of this collection – not picking and choosing, but absorbing the entire discussion here – we could help to change the trajectory of this history. We can do this, I think, only if we are willing to unmask 'gender'. We will have to pull away gender's reassuring public mask of comfortable blandness and reveal it for what it should be: a conceptual tool to make us see things at work that we would rather not see.

APPENDIX I

Windhoek Declaration

On the 10th Anniversary of the United Nations Transitional Assistance Group (UNTAG)
Windhoek, Namibia, 31 May 2000

In a world riven by war, women and men yearn for peace and are everywhere striving to resolve conflict and bring about peace, reconciliation and stability in their communities, their countries and through the United Nations and regional organizations.

United Nations peace operations have evolved from peacekeeping, in its traditional sense, towards multidimensional peace support operations. So far, women have been denied their full role in these efforts, both nationally and internationally, and the gender dimension in peace processes has not been adequately addressed.

In order to ensure the effectiveness of peace support operations, the principles of gender equality must permeate the entire mission, at all levels, thus ensuring the participation of women and men as equal partners and beneficiaries in all aspects of the peace process – from peacekeeping, reconciliation and peace-building, towards a situation of political stability in which women and men play an equal part in the political, economic and social development of their country.

Having considered these matters in Windhoek, Namibia, at a seminar on 'Mainstreaming a Gender Perspective in Multidimensional Peace Support Operations' organized by the Lessons Learned Unit of the UN Department of Peacekeeping Operations and hosted by the Government of Namibia from 29 to 31 May 2000, participants looked at practical ways in which the UN system and Member States can bring the aims set out above closer to realization. In that regard, the Seminar recommends 'The Namibia Plan of Action' and urges the Secretary-General to ensure that appropriate follow-up measures are taken to implement it, in consultation with Member States, and that periodic progress reviews are undertaken.

NAMIBIA PLAN OF ACTION ON MAINSTREAMING A GENDER PERSPECTIVE IN MULTIDIMENSIONAL PEACE SUPPORT OPERATIONS

1. Negotiations in Furtherance of a Ceasefire and/or Peace Agreements:

- Equal access and participation by women and men should be ensured in the area of conflict at all levels and stages of the peace process.
- In negotiations for a ceasefire and/or peace agreements, women should be an integral part of the negotiating team and process. The negotiating team and/or facilitators should ensure that gender issues are placed on the agenda and that those issues are addressed fully in the agreement.

2. Mandate

- The initial assessment mission for any peace support operation should include a senior adviser on gender mainstreaming.
- The Secretary-General's initial report to the Security Council, based on the assessment mission, should include the issue of gender mainstreaming, and should propose adequate budgetary provisions.
- Security Council resolutions setting up and extending peace support operations should incorporate a specific mandate on gender mainstreaming.
- All mandates for peace support operations should refer to the provisions of the Convention on the Elimination of All Forms of Discrimination against Women, as well as other relevant international legal instruments.
- Follow-on mechanisms should be established within the mission's mandate to carry over tasks to implement fully gender mainstreaming in the post-conflict reconstruction period.

3. Leadership

- In accordance with the Secretary-General's target of 50 per cent women in managerial and decision-making positions, more determined efforts must be made to select and appoint female Special Representatives of the Secretary-General and senior field staff for peace support operations.
- A comprehensive database with information specifically on female candidates with their qualifications, both military and civilian, should be maintained.
- An Advisory Board should be set up within the Department of

Peacekeeping Operations (DPKO), preferably with qualified external participation, to ensure that this database and existing lists of female candidates are given due consideration.

- Special Representatives of the Secretary-General and senior mission personnel should receive an in-depth briefing on gender mainstreaming issues prior to deployment.

4. Planning, Structure and Resources of Missions

- A gender affairs unit is crucial for effective gender mainstreaming and should be a standard component of all missions. It should be adequately funded and staffed at appropriate levels and should have direct access to senior decision-makers.
- The DPKO-led operational planning teams at United Nations Headquarters must include gender specialists and representatives of other United Nations agencies and organizations dealing with gender issues.
- All DPKO and Department of Political Affairs briefings to the Security Council, as well as formal and informal briefings to the General Assembly legislative bodies, Member States and other relevant bodies, should integrate gender issues related to that particular mission.
- There is a need for the financial authorities of the United Nations, particularly the Advisory Committee on Administrative and Budgetary Questions, to give priority to the funding of gender mainstreaming.
- Lessons learned from current and prior missions on gender should be incorporated at the planning stage of a new mission. To this end, the compilation of good practices on gender mainstreaming should be constantly updated.

5. Recruitment

- The United Nations must set an example by rapidly increasing the number of senior female civilian personnel in peace support operations in all relevant Headquarters departments, including DPKO, and in the field.
- Member States should be asked to increase the number of women in their military and civilian police forces who are qualified to serve in peace support operations at all levels, including the most senior. To this end, a stronger mechanism than the current *note verbale* to troop-contributing nations should be developed. Requests to troop-contributing nations

could be tailor-made to nations that are known to have suitable female staff, while other potential troop-contributing nations could be encouraged to develop longer-term strategies to increase the number and rank of female personnel in their respective forces.

- The terms of reference, including eligibility requirements, for all heads of mission components and their personnel should be reviewed and modified to facilitate the increased participation of women, and, depending on the outcome of that review, special measures should be taken to secure this goal.
- All agreements and individual contracts governing the assignment of personnel, including arrangements for United Nations Volunteers, should reflect the gender-related obligations and responsibilities of those personnel. In particular, the code of conduct should be addressed in all of these documents.

6. Training

- Troop-contributing nations, which are training military, police and civilian personnel specifically for their participation in peace support operations, should involve a higher percentage of women in that training.
- Gender issues should be mainstreamed throughout all regional and national training curricula and courses for peace support operations, particularly those sponsored directly by the Training Unit of DPKO.
- In order to meet United Nations standards for behaviour, DPKO should provide gender awareness guidelines and materials so that Member States can incorporate these elements into their national training programmes for military and civilian police personnel in preparation for deployment. Such training should be enhanced by United Nations Training Assistance Teams and train-the-trainers programmes.
- Obligatory induction training with regard to gender issues held upon arrival at mission areas should include the following:

  Code of Conduct;

  Culture, history and social norms of the host country;

  Convention on the Elimination of All Forms of Discrimination against Women; and

  Sexual harassment and sexual assault.

7. Procedures

- DPKO should consider the gender mainstreaming mechanisms currently used by United Nations agencies and adopt an appropriate version for their field operations. DPKO directives should be amended to include gender mainstreaming.
- The reporting mechanisms between the field and Headquarters on gender mainstreaming need to be clarified.
- A post for a Senior Gender Adviser in DPKO, to serve as gender focal point for field missions, should be funded under the regular budget or the peacekeeping support account and filled as a matter of urgency.
- The terms of reference of the Senior Gender Adviser should ensure a proper interchange of information and experience between gender units in individual missions.
- The functions and roles of mission gender units/advisers should be announced to all personnel.
- Standard Operating Procedures applying to all components of missions should be developed on the issues of sexual assault and sexual harassment.

8. Monitoring, Evaluation and Accountability

- Accountability for all issues relating to gender mainstreaming at the field level should be vested at the highest level, in the Secretary-General's Special Representative, who should be assigned the responsibility of ensuring that gender mainstreaming is implemented in all areas and components of the mission.
- The Special Committee on Peacekeeping Operations and other concerned legislative bodies should submit recommendations to the General Assembly promoting gender mainstreaming in peace operations.
- Monitoring and evaluation mechanisms to assess the implementation of the United Nations gender mainstreaming objectives should be established at United Nations Headquarters and at peacekeeping missions, in consultation with the Office of the Special Adviser on Gender Issues and Advancement of Women.
- The current format of reporting, particularly with regard to situation reports and periodic reports of the Secretary-General, should include progress on gender mainstreaming throughout peacekeeping missions.

- There should be periodic and end-of-mission evaluations, led by an independent external team, of the degree to which the United Nations gender mainstreaming approach and objectives have been integrated into all policies and activities of each peace support operation. The first studies should be on East Timor and Kosovo.
- Reporting mechanisms should be established to monitor the effects of the implementation of the peace agreement on the host country population from a gender perspective.
- Research should be encouraged on the short- and long-term effects of the gender dimension of peace support operations on the host country population. Such research should be designed to strengthen host country research capacity, in particular that of women researchers.

9. Public Awareness

All possible means should be employed to increase public awareness of the importance of gender mainstreaming in peace support operations. In this connection, the media should play a significant and positive role.

APPENDIX II

United Nations Resolution 1325 (2000)

Adopted by the Security Council at its 4213th meeting
on 31 October 2000

The Security Council,

Recalling its resolutions 1261 (1999) of 25 August 1999, 1265 (1999) of 17 September 1999, 1296 (2000) of 19 April 2000 and 1314 (2000) of 11 August 2000, as well as relevant statements of its President, and

Recalling also the statement of its President to the press on the occasion of the United Nations Day for Women's Rights and International Peace (International Women's Day) of 8 March 2000 (SC/6816),

Recalling also the commitments of the Beijing Declaration and Platform for Action (A/52/231) as well as those contained in the outcome document of the twenty-third Special Session of the United Nations General Assembly entitled 'Women 2000: Gender Equality, Development and Peace for the Twenty-First Century' (A/S-23/10/Rev.1), in particular those concerning women and armed conflict,

Bearing in mind the purposes and principles of the Charter of the United Nations and the primary responsibility of the Security Council under the Charter for the maintenance of international peace and security,

Expressing concern that civilians, particularly women and children, account for the vast majority of those adversely affected by armed conflict, including as refugees and internally displaced persons, and increasingly are targeted by combatants and armed elements, and

Recognizing the consequent impact this has on durable peace and reconciliation,

Reaffirming the important role of women in the prevention and resolution of conflicts and in peace-building, and

Stressing the importance of their equal participation and full involvement in all efforts for the maintenance and promotion of peace and security, and the need to increase their role in decision-making with regard to conflict prevention and resolution,

Reaffirming also the need to implement fully international humanitarian and human rights law that protects the rights of women and girls during and after conflicts,

Emphasizing the need for all parties to ensure that mine clearance and mine awareness programmes take into account the special needs of women and girls,

Recognizing the urgent need to mainstream a gender perspective into peacekeeping operations, and in this regard *noting* the Windhoek Declaration and the Namibia Plan of Action on Mainstreaming a Gender Perspective in Multidimensional Peace Support Operations (S/2000/693),

Recognizing also the importance of the recommendation contained in the statement of its President to the press of 8 March 2000 for specialized training for all peacekeeping personnel on the protection, special needs and human rights of women and children in conflict situations,

Recognizing that an understanding of the impact of armed conflict on women and girls, effective institutional arrangements to guarantee their protection and full participation in the peace process can significantly contribute to the maintenance and promotion of international peace and security,

Noting the need to consolidate data on the impact of armed conflict on women and girls,

1. *Urges* Member States to ensure increased representation of women at all decision-making levels in national, regional and international institutions and mechanisms for the prevention, management, and resolution of conflict;

2. *Encourages* the Secretary-General to implement his strategic plan of action (A/49/587) calling for an increase in the participation of women at decision-making levels in conflict resolution and peace processes;

3. *Urges* the Secretary-General to appoint more women as special representatives and envoys to pursue good offices on his behalf, and in this regard *calls on* Member States to provide candidates to the Secretary-General, for inclusion in a regularly updated centralized roster;

4. *Further urges* the Secretary-General to seek to expand the role and contribution of women in United Nations field-based operations, and especially among military observers, civilian police, human rights and humanitarian personnel;

5. *Expresses* its willingness to incorporate a gender perspective into peacekeeping operations, and *urges* the Secretary-General to ensure that, where appropriate, field operations include a gender component;

6. *Requests* the Secretary-General to provide to Member States training guidelines and materials on the protection, rights and the particular needs of women, as well as on the importance of involving women in all peacekeeping and peace-building measures, *invites* Member States to incorporate these elements as well as HIV/AIDS awareness training into their national training programmes for military and civilian police personnel in preparation for deployment, and *further requests* the Secretary-General to ensure that civilian personnel of peacekeeping operations receive similar training;

7. *Urges* Member States to increase their voluntary financial, technical and logistical support for gender-sensitive training efforts, including those undertaken by relevant funds and programmes, inter alia, the United Nations Fund for Women and United Nations Children's Fund, and by the Office of the United Nations High Commissioner for Refugees and other relevant bodies;

8. *Calls on* all actors involved, when negotiating and implementing peace agreements, to adopt a gender perspective, including, inter alia:

   (a) The special needs of women and girls during repatriation and resettlement and for rehabilitation, reintegration and post-conflict reconstruction;

   (b) Measures that support local women's peace initiatives and indigenous processes for conflict resolution, and that involve women in all of the implementation mechanisms of the peace agreements;

   (c) Measures that ensure the protection of and respect for human rights of women and girls, particularly as they relate to the constitution, the electoral system, the police and the judiciary;

9. *Calls upon* all parties to armed conflict to respect fully international law applicable to the rights and protection of women and girls, especially as civilians, in particular the obligations applicable to them under the Geneva Conventions of 1949 and the Additional Protocols thereto of 1977, the Refugee Convention of 1951 and the Protocol thereto of 1967, the Convention on the Elimination of All Forms of Discrimination against Women of 1979 and the Optional Protocol thereto of 1999 and the United Nations Convention on the Rights of the Child of 1989 and the two Optional Protocols thereto of 25 May 2000, and to bear in mind the relevant provisions of the Rome Statute of the International Criminal Court;

10. *Calls on* all parties to armed conflict to take special measures to protect women and girls from gender-based violence, particularly rape and other forms of sexual abuse, and all other forms of violence in situations of armed conflict;

11. *Emphasizes* the responsibility of all States to put an end to impunity and to prosecute those responsible for genocide, crimes against humanity, and war crimes including those relating to sexual and other violence against women and girls, and in this regard *stresses* the need to exclude these crimes, where feasible from amnesty provisions;

12. *Calls upon* all parties to armed conflict to respect the civilian and humanitarian character of refugee camps and settlements, and to take into account the particular needs of women and girls, including in their design, and recalls its resolutions 1208 (1998) of 19 November 1998 and 1296 (2000) of 19 April 2000;

13. *Encourages* all those involved in the planning for disarmament, demobilization and reintegration to consider the different needs of female and male ex-combatants and to take into account the needs of their dependants;

14. *Reaffirms* its readiness, whenever measures are adopted under Article 41 of the Charter of the United Nations, to give consideration to their potential impact on the civilian population, bearing in mind the special needs of women and girls, in order to consider appropriate humanitarian exemptions;

15. *Expresses* its willingness to ensure that Security Council missions take into account gender considerations and the rights of women, including through consultation with local and international women's groups;

16. *Invites* the Secretary-General to carry out a study on the impact of armed conflict on women and girls, the role of women in peace-building and the gender dimensions of peace processes and conflict resolution, and *further invites* him to submit a report to the Security Council on the results of this study and to make this available to all Member States of the United Nations;

17. *Requests* the Secretary-General, where appropriate, to include in his reporting to the Security Council progress on gender mainstreaming throughout peacekeeping missions and all other aspects relating to women and girls;

18. *Decides* to remain actively seized of the matter.

APPENDIX III

Gendering Human Security: From Marginalization to the Integration of Women in Peacebuilding

Recommendations for policy and practice from the NUPI–Fafo Forum on Gender Relations in Post-Conflict Transitions

The Seminar

On 24–26 January 2001 the Norwegian Institute of International Affairs (NUPI) and the Programme for International Co-operation and Conflict Resolution (PIC-CR) of the Fafo Institute for Applied Social Science held a learning seminar, or Forum, on Gender Relations in Post-conflict Transitions. The organization of the Forum was led by NUPI and the meeting was held at the Fafo Institute in Oslo.

The purpose of the Forum was to develop an understanding of gender and decision making in post-conflict transitions and identify relevant recommendations for practitioners on how to integrate women in the peacebuilding process. The Forum asked the following questions: How have women contributed to the survival of parts of the civil and physical infrastructure? What has been the experience of women decision-makers in the transition from conflict? Has there been a process of marginalization and, if so, how has it occurred? What has been the impact of peacebuilding assistance on women in general and their roles in politics and decision making in particular? How can international organizations help to empower women in post-conflict societies? If the focus was on women, the ultimate aim of the debate was to improve the basis for viable peaceful solution to conflicts to the benefit of the total society, both women and men, elderly and children.

The Forum gathered more than 40 people from international organizations, governments, NGOs and universities and research institutes. Participants were invited on the basis of their experience of policy processes and programme implementation in the relevant multilateral or national arenas, including several participants from countries in conflict or emerging from conflict. The organizers are grateful for this great interest and are pleased that the high number of participants, and the different backgrounds which they have brought to bear on the subject, has generated an outcome which includes both analytical perspectives as well as a number of concrete recommendations.

The Report

This Appendix contains the Preface and Recommendations of the Forum report, which was prepared by Kari Karame, Researcher, NUPI, with the assistance of Gudrun Bertinussen. The report is a joint NUPI-Fafo publication, and it is based on the various experiences, views and recommendations expressed by the participants during the Oslo Forum. The intention of the Forum was to explore the complexity of the questions posed, while simultaneously seeking to elaborate concrete recommendations for strengthening policy and practice. The report is intended to reflect the views expressed during the Forum, but it is not a consensus document and the views recorded here are not necessarily those of the authors, their institutions nor of the participants.

Preface

The nature of wars has changed radically during the last two decades. Most of today's armed conflicts are internal, which means that they take place within the borders of one state, though they may often spill over into the neighbouring states. The populations of such intrastate wars are usually of different ethnic and/or religious identity and often it is the national, cultural, historical or religious identity of the state which is at stake. These circumstances place an increased importance on the cultural sensitivity of international assistance provided to societies emerging from conflict.

The particularities of conflict are unique, but many conflicts share several characteristics. The state apparatus is weakened or has collapsed totally, and the parties in conflict will therefore have great power over their own people. The distinction between the military and the civilian fields is blurred, and likewise between the battlefront and the home front. As adult men often face the choice of either fleeing or fighting, women may have to take on responsibilities and roles that they were not prepared for by the traditional gendered pattern of behaviour.

The civilian population has become the main target of warfare, and 80 to 85 per cent of the victims are civilians. Sexual violence against women is used as a strategy of war, and is recognized as a crime against humanity. Women, children and elderly make up the majority of the refugees and the internally displaced persons. As a result, human security or the protection of civilians has become a major focus for international intervention and assistance.

During these conflicts women are victims and survivors, but also fighters and participants, leaders and activists. Women are often primarily responsible for maintaining the core relationships and functions in society, at home, as refugees or as displaced persons. In this sense, therefore, war also offers possibilities for the empowerment of women. This empowerment is, in turn, crucial to re-launching the social and economic development at the core of many peacebuilding strategies.

Yet, societies emerging from conflict may experience a redefinition of the role and status of women in society, resulting in the marginalization or isolation of women from the key peacebuilding processes in the transition from conflict. And thereby the tremendous knowledge and capacity resources that women have developed during conflict are either lost or neglected.

Recommendations

Local Context

I. Local Knowledge

- Different conflicts have different dynamics and characteristics which international assistance should take into consideration prior to implementation.
- While the policies and practices of international assistance should integrate local knowledge, stereotypical and essentialist views of local conditions concerning women's abilities and potentials should be avoided.
- Gender- and culture-sensitive programmes are enhanced when local women's knowledge of the needs and conditions of society is recognized as a resource. This knowledge should be integrated into the planning of assistance, including support to institution building, democratization, protection of human rights, as well as through peacekeeping missions or the provision of humanitarian aid. In the field, one way to achieve this should include co-operation with existing women's networks.
- International human rights standards should remain a point of reference for the planners and implementers of assistance.

II. Jurisdiction

- In general, attention should be paid to the fact that in many countries emerging from conflict women are not individual legal persons or are in other administrative ways prevented from full participation in the reconstruction of society.

- The political negotiations at the heart of peace processes should address women's rights, including property and land rights. Often in post-conflict situations widows are not able to inherit or assume title over the land, property, benefits, incentives or entitlements of their deceased husbands or male relatives. Wives of disappeared men may be denied access to title deeds for many years.
- Women should be provided with passports or ID cards to enable them to register and be eligible for assistance.
- Election laws should ensure that women are not excluded from political participation, taking into consideration the particularity of the local social conditions as one electoral paradigm will not fit all.

III. Personal Security

- Post-conflict societies often suffer from lawlessness, including domestic violence. Special attention should therefore be paid to women's personal security in such situations.
- The planning and implementation of international assistance should pay particular attention to women's needs when planning and establishing refugee camps and in the facilitation of the return of displaced persons.
- The traumatized victims of sexual violence during a conflict will need special care during and immediately after violent conflict.
- Gender awareness training should be integrated to the training of international staff deployed in post-conflict situations, including civilian police, law enforcement and social security personnel, as well as peacekeepers (soldiers) and heads of missions.
- Troop contributing states and donor countries should promote women as mission officers and as heads of missions. Women members of international missions tend to be more sensitive to the needs of local women, and local women often find it easier to communicate with other women.

IV. Political Participation

- Training should be provided for women who wish to become active in organized politics or for women who wish to expand their impact within established political organizations.
- To assure women's participation in political life, both as voters and as activists, quotas for women candidates in post-conflict elections should

be advocated by international electoral authorities. These should be considered in light of local capacities and conditions.

- To be effective, quotas will require that training be provided to political candidates prior to elections and on an on-going basis.
- Local women's organizations should be asked to play a lead role in the process of political capacity-building. Such organizations could also provide a forum for women if their voices are excluded from existing political parties or fora.
- Women should be trained for political lobby work. Specific resources should be dedicated to the training of women in advocacy (lobbying) work and for women parliamentarians.

V. Reintegration of Combatants

- The repatriation and the social reintegration of ex-combatants – both men and women – is a delicate process with potentially significant implications for a society emerging from conflict. Special support programmes are needed to ease this process, as in some cases former combatants have turned to criminal activities and violence in the absence of a social network to assist them in re-integration.
- Special programmes are needed to address the potential for domestic violence. These programmes should target men who are being reintegrated as, during conflict, men are often socialized into a culture of violence.

The Global Context

VI. Early Warning

- A growing lack of security for civilians is often one of the indicators of an impending armed conflict. Early warning systems should be further developed, based on indicators that take into account the insecurity of women, the elderly and children.

VII. International Law

- International law, including international human rights and humanitarian law, does provide for the protection of women. However, there is a problem of enforcement. In most cases, troop contributing states and donor countries participating in peace or humanitarian missions are required by law to ensure the compliance with international law of the parties to the conflict. To limit impunity, these states should act through the appropriate enforcement mechanisms to ensure that special attention is paid to those violations of the law designed to protect women.

VIII. Peace Processes

- The Facilitators of peace negotiations should work to ensure that women from all levels of society, are part of the peace process. They should help to provide space for advocacy and lobbying in order to avoid the isolation or exclusion of women.
- Peace processes should include frameworks that take into account the needs of women, the elderly and children. Central to such frameworks should be mechanisms to ensure that the views of women are taken into consideration at all stages of the peace process, from the planning and framing of a mandate to the implementation of a peace agreement.
- Peace efforts in exile communities should be supported as the refugees, both men and women, are also part of the peace process, and may influence its course.
- Training should be made available to women and women's organizations to facilitate their participation peace processes which are held outside the local context (e.g. training in English, law, etc.).

IX. Co-ordination between International Actors

- Co-ordination between local, national, regional, bilateral and multilateral organizations, including NGOs, in the planning, design and implementation of projects should bring together gender advisors in the field to advise headquarters and capitals level policy makers on appropriate policies.

X. Gender Training within International Agencies

- International organizations should not ask a war-torn society to implement gender balance if this principle has yet to be implemented within the organizations themselves. International implementation agencies should be transparent and accountable for their own operationalization of gender balance.
- Training in gender awareness is important for middle management but should not be restricted to one gender advisor or the organization's gender unit.
- Gender training should also be provided to senior management in international agencies before their entering field positions.

- These internal initiatives will require the allocation of resources to gender-sensitive programming.

XI. Peacekeeping

- In the interests of the success of a mission, the contributing countries should work to ensure a greater representation of women in all stages and on all levels of peacekeeping missions.
- Relations between peacekeepers and the local population can depend upon the sensitivity of personnel to local norms and expectations. Peacekeepers – both women and men – should be trained in gender awareness. The focus should be on cultural sensitivity as the norms for interaction between men and women vary from one society to another.
- Mission mandates should include reference to codes of conduct for peacekeepers as concerns contact with local women and women's personal security. Codes of conduct for peacekeepers should include specific provisions prohibiting prostitution.

XII. International Assistance

- International assistance should respect local agendas.
- Co-ordination should seek to pool resources linking the many actors working in the field to pull in the same direction.
- Policies should be linked to timetables to ensure implementation.
- Local qualified women must be included in the field offices in positions of authority and not only as translators.

XIII. Accountability

- Systems of benchmarking, evaluation and accountability of international activities should be developed with regard to both gender awareness and gender balance.

XIV. Strategies for Implementation

- The United Nations system, regional organizations and international NGOs are all to some extent dependent upon policy decisions made in the capitals of member states and donor countries. The focus of advocacy should be on these governments with the demand that they implement or support the implementation of the recommendations for gender mainstreaming and gender awareness.

- Similarly, coalitions of 'like-minded' member states – such as the Human Security Network or parallel coalitions of NGOs – should promote gender main-streaming and gender awareness within implementation agencies.

- Another focus for policy advocacy is the upcoming report on and implementation of UNSC Resolution 1325. Policy formulation processes as a result of Resolution 1325 are already underway and in this context participants urged practitioners and policy makers to consider the work undertaken during the Forum and in previous meetings (e.g. Windhoek, Uppsala, etc.). It was suggested that the formation of a group of 'Friends' of Resolution 1325 may help provide a focal point for input from member states and NGOs.

- Finally, the on-going follow-up to the Report on Strengthening UN Peace Operations (Brahimi Report) provides an opportunity for member states to integrate gender awareness and gender mainstreaming to the reform of UN peace operations. Forum participants noted that the Brahimi report was silent on the question of gender and that the follow-up policy formulation processes underway at the UN offered an opportunity to correct the absence of gender analysis in the report.

Abstracts

The Idea of Women in Peacekeeping: Lysistrata and Antigone *by Mary-Jane Fox*

The relatively recent concept and practice of peacekeeping have been a predominantly male concern, like war and military matters in general. Efforts to introduce gender mainstreaming into peacekeeping missions are notable, yet they are long overdue and hardly a new idea. Two ancient Greek plays, *Antigone* and *Lysistrata*, challenge both past and contemporary objections to women's involvement in matters of peacekeeping as well as the negative stereotyping of women upon which those objections are based. In doing so, they also lend some support to the contemporary notion of essentialism and women's 'natural' predisposition to be nurturing, non-aggressive and conciliatory. They might also, however, serve as evidence for the durability of the constructivist perspective over time. No matter which approach is taken, however, the fact remains that for centuries women have been relegated to the private sphere of life, and paradoxically seem to have acquired attributes which are relevant in the public and predominantly male domain of peacekeeping today.

A Few Good Women: Gender Stereotypes, the Military and Peacekeeping *by Gerard J. DeGroot*

Gender stereotypes of peaceful, nurturing women, common to almost all cultures, have traditionally limited the participation of women in the military and in combat. When women have participated in war, by subterfuge or in an emergency, their contribution has subsequently been discounted in order to limit the effect upon gender dynamics. Thus, though women have participated in war, their participation has not brought privileges of citizenship in the way male service often has. Advocates of gender integration in the military have tried to refute the validity of gender stereotypes, arguing that women, through effective training, can become efficient soldiers. Lately, however, the increased deployment of military units in peacekeeping operations has led to an appreciation of the qualities women supposedly possess – regardless of whether they are genetically or socially determined. Thus, militaries of the future might want women for the very same reasons they have rejected them in the past.

Women, Peacekeeping and Peacemaking: Gender Balance and Mainstreaming *by Judith Hicks Stiehm*

Until the end of the Cold War peacekeeping was primarily a UN, a military, and a male enterprise. In its classical, Nobel Prize-winning form the UN's Blue Helmets assumed their military observing and monitoring duties only with the consent of the opposing forces, observed strict neutrality between them, and used force only for self-defence and as a last resort. In the last decade different operations referred to as peacekeeping have violated each of these tenets. Further, the responsibilities of peacekeepers greatly expanded to include humanitarian relief, refugee return, demining, civilian policing, demobilization, human rights monitoring, elections, and nation building. These new activities directly affect women. And women clearly have the capacity to participate in and even direct these new activities. Recognizing this, the UN has established policies related to gender balance and gender mainstreaming which apply to all UN components including peacekeeping operations. To implement and institutionalize these new policies will require commitment, resources and sound strategies to overcome institutional inertia and, sometimes, resistance.

'Women and Peace and Security': The Politics of Implementing Gender Sensitivity Norms in Peacekeeping *by Henry F. Carey*

A new international regime mandating mainstreaming gender responsiveness and women's rights in peace negotiations and complex UN peacekeeping was consolidated in October 2000 with the UN Security Council's hearings on the subject and Resolution 1325 legally requiring multitudinous initiatives. While women's rights, including universal jurisdiction covering sexual violence, were already part of this regime, the programmatic endeavours became legally binding as a result of this resolution. These include involving women's NGOs and women in official capacities in both negotiations to make peace and the implementation of peacebuilding. This contribution outlines the development of various norms (both those which are directly part of the regime and others which affect it) that are legally binding, as well as policy and programmatic initiatives whose makeup is developed on a case-by-case basis. It calls attention to the difficulties of implementing them by reviewing problems of protecting women's rights and related human rights norms in both treaty-based and UN Charter-based bodies.

Sexual Violence in Times of War: A New Challenge for Peace Operations? *by Inger Skjelsbæk*

One of the new aspects of warfare that peacekeepers need to grapple with is the systematic use of sexual violence for political purposes. The war in Bosnia and Herzegovina and the genocide in Rwanda are cases in point. This contribution provides an outline of the use of sexual violence in times of war, based on a survey of sources carried out in 1998. It attempts to explain how sexual violence in war can be conceptualized and how it has been described in various conflict areas in articles written in the 1990s. Also, the contribution presents findings on the effect of wartime sexual violence and then discusses the challenges this particular form of violence creates for peace operations.

Military Women in Peace Operations: Experiences of the Norwegian Battalion in UNIFIL 1978–98 *by Kari H. Karamé*

For 20 years Norway participated in the United Nation's peacekeeping forces in South Lebanon. On average there were 30 women in each contingent, which consisted of up to 900 persons. During the first years they served in the medical corps, logistics and staff units. In 1984 full gender equality was introduced in the Norwegian armed forces, and from then on a growing number of women also served in military posts in South Lebanon. In 1992, a Swedish Major-General took over as force commander. One of his initiatives was to recommend the exclusion of women from most military functions, a decision based on the assumption that they could not perform their duties because of the presence of Muslim men. This initiated an intense discussion in Norway, revealing some of the contradictions that may occur within a multinational force between the intentions of UN headquarters, different nations' policies and the reality in the field. It also presented an opportunity to debate women's contribution to peace operations.

Gender Mainstreaming in Practice: The United Nations Transitional Assistance Group in Namibia *by Louise Olsson*

The process of developing a policy for gender-adapted, or mainstreamed, multidimensional peacekeeping operations has been erratic in the UN. However, in 1989, the UN operation in Namibia, United Nations Transitional Assistance Group (UNTAG), had already started to develop practices for gender mainstreaming of the civilian sector of the operation. UNTAG's civilian component was fairly gender balanced and some of the UN civilian staff were adapting their work in order to reach both women and men in the Namibian population. This contribution discusses the lessons that could have been learned about gender mainstreaming in the Namibian case and on which a contemporary UN gender mainstreaming policy could have been based. This concerns methods of increasing female UN staff, mobilizing local women to vote, incorporation of issues of equality in the constitution, and the importance of leadership in enhancing equality and equity.

Notes on Contributors

Henry F. Carey is Assistant Professor of Political Science at Georgia State University, where he teaches international politics, organization and law. He has edited *National Reconciliation in Eastern Europe* (2001) and *Politics and Society in Post-Communist Romania* (2001), and has published articles on humanitarian intervention, human rights and transitional elections.

Gerard J. DeGroot is Professor and Head of the Department of Modern History at the University of St Andrews in Scotland. He has published eight books and numerous articles on war and the military, including *A Soldier and A Woman: Sexual Integration in the Military* (2000) and *The First World War* (2001).

Cynthia Enloe is Professor of Government at Clark University and author of *The Morning After: Sexual Politics at the End of the Cold War* (California, 1993), *Bananas, Beaches and Bases: Making Feminist Sense of International Politics* (California, 1990), and *Does Kaki Become You?* (1988).

Mary-Jane Fox is a Researcher and Lecturer at the Department of Peace and Conflict Research, Uppsala University, Sweden. Her most recent publications are 'Somalia Divided: The African Cerberus (Considerations on Political Culture)', *Civil Wars*, Spring 1999, and 'Missing the Boat to Self-Determination: Palestine and Namibia in Retrospect', *Arab Studies Quarterly*, Summer 1998.

Kari H. Karamé is Senior Researcher at the Norwegian Institute of International Affairs (NUPI). Her major interests are the general security situation in Lebanon, Syria and Jordan and issues concerning gender, conflict and war. Her latest publication, edited with Torunn L. Tryggestad, is *Gender Perspectives on Peace and Conflict Studies* (2000). She holds a Mag.Art. in Ethnology from the University of Oslo. She has lived in Lebanon for many years and taught at the American University of Beirut, the Lebanese University and at St. Joseph University, where she was head of the Department for Ethnology and Anthropology.

Louise Olsson is a PhD candidate at the Department of Peace and Conflict Research at Uppsala University, Sweden. She was an associate of the United Nation's Project 'Mainstreaming a Gender Perspective in Multidimensional Peace Support Operations'. She wrote two reports related to this project, one published by the Department of Peace and Conflict Research and one by the Lessons Learned Unit of the Department of Peacekeeping Operations at the UN. She published an article on gender and peacekeeping in *International Peacekeeping*, Autumn 2000.

Inger Skjelsbæk holds an M.Phil. in social psychology. She is a Researcher at the International Peace Research Institute, Oslo (PRIO), and is currently working on a doctoral project on the social memory of the mass rapes during the war in Bosnia and Herzegovina. Her latest publications include *Gender, Peace and Conflict*, edited with Dan Smith (2001).

Judith Hicks Stiehm is Professor of Political Science at Florida International University where she served as Provost and Academic Vice-President for four years. She has taught at the University of Wisconsin, UCLA, and the University of Southern California. She has been a Visiting Professor at the US Army Peacekeeping Institute and at the Strategic Studies Institute at Carlisle Barracks. Her books include *Nonviolent Power: Active and Passive Resistance*, *Bring Me Men and Women: Mandated Change at the U.S. Air Force Academy*, *Arms and the Enlisted Woman* and *It*'s *Our Military Too!* Stiehm has served on the Defense Advisory Committee on Women in the Military, as a consultant to the United Nations Commission for the Advancement of Women and to the Lessons Learned Unit of the Department of Peacekeeping Operations. She is a member of the Council on Foreign Relations, holds the US Army Distinguished Civilian Service Medal and appears in the most recent edition of *Who's Who*.

Torunn L. Tryggestad is a project co-ordinator at the Programme on Peacekeeping and Multinational Operations (UN Programme), The Norwegian Institute of International Affairs (NUPI). She was Acting Director of the UN Programme from March to December 2000. She holds an M.Phil. in political science from the University of Oslo. Her main area of interest is in peacekeeping capacity-building in Africa, and she has been working with the Training for Peace in Southern Africa Project since 1995. Her latest publication, edited with Kari Karamé, is *Gender Perspectives on Peace and Conflict Studies* (2000).

Index

THE EVOLUTION OF US PEACEKEEPING POLICY UNDER CLINTON

A Fairweather Friend?

Michael MacKinnon, *Graduate Institute of International Studies, Geneva*

This timely analysis will be of great impact in the study of US–UN relations and US peacekeeping policy, as well as providing an interesting window on the mind of a President.

224 pages 1999
0 7146 4937 6 cloth
0 7146 4497 8 paper
Cass Series on Peacekeeping No. 6

PEACEKEEPING AND PUBLIC INFORMATION

Caught in the Crossfire

Ingrid A Lehmann, *Director, United Nations Information Centre, Athens*

> *'Peacekeeping and Public Information...proves how important an understanding of peace operations mounted by the UN is.'*
>
> **Linda Melvern, *Glasgow Herald (Books of the Year)***

192 pages maps 1999
0 7146 4930 9 cloth
0 7146 4490 0 paper
Cass Series on Peacekeeping No. 5

BEYOND THE EMERGENCY

Development Within UN Peace Missions

Jeremy Ginifer, *Norwegian Institute of International Affairs* (Ed)

> *'The book makes a noteworthy addition to writings on UN conflict resolution, peacekeeping and peace building by exploring the often-neglected nature of development and when and how this feature – as a continuing long-term objective and end in itself – should fit into these processes.'*
>
> ***Journal of Peace Research***

152 pages 1997
0 7146 4760 8 cloth
0 7146 4321 1 paper
Cass Series on Peacekeeping No 1
A special issue of the journal International Peacekeeping